The Trump Card

The Trump Card

American Constitutional Crisis,
Roman Dictators, and the Neoimperial Presidency

Rajeev S. Sreetharan

The Trump Card: American Constitutional Crisis, Roman Dictators, and the Neoimperial Presidency by Rajeev S. Sreetharan

www.rajeevss.io

Book Cover Design and Illustration by Sam Wall
www.samwall.com

E-book and Print Formatting by Maureen Cutajar
www.gopublished.com

In the course of this book, I allege that certain government officials are responsible for violating various provisions of international humanitarian law, international human rights law, or the Constitution of the United States. These assertions constitute my opinions based on the facts, reasoning, and political and legal history I set forth in the text.

The illustrations within this volume were created by the author.

ISBN: 978-0-692-77659-9

Sapere Aude

Table of Contents

1

Black Swan to Trojan Horse

black swan event*blak–swän–i-vent*\\
(n.) An unpredictable or unforeseen event, typically one
with extreme consequences that are rationalized after
the fact as explainable and predictable.[1]

Take a breath. And take it *all* in.

Here and now, we breathe in the belly of a unique historical moment, one that has *never* confronted an American electorate before and one that we will *never* confront again.

Before our eyes, America's *first* black presidency of the White House winds down, the domicile of only well-to-do white male presidents since 1789. The Democratic Party officially nominated Hillary R. Clinton, its *first* female presidential candidate since the founding of the political party in 1828. It is also the very *first* time (and with all reasonable probability the *very* last) that ex-President Bill Clinton and ex-model Melania Trump will submit an application to the American people for the same position. And then we have Donald Trump, a political outsider who, for the *first* time in world history, seems to have truly subverted the presidential election season of a democratic superpower into a dicey game of Russian roulette.

As a voter, if you are not even mildly petrified of the idea of a Trump presidency as November 8th nears, keep reading.

A veritable Goliath in the business realm, Trump makes for an ironic David in presidential politics. Remember in 2015 when he *was* an underdog? No more. Once a punch line, the multibillionaire real estate mogul with a sixth-grade vocabulary is now a viable *and* competitive presidential candidate, contending for the big prize held by George Washington and John Adams, Richard Nixon and Barack Obama. In true underdog fashion, Trump has defied all odds, securing the official Republican nomination on July 19th, 2016.

As well-to-do and as white as can be, Trump is a black swan candidate. The savvy mercantilist of bottled water and luxury hotels now desires to add 1600 Pennsylvania Avenue to his real estate portfolio and himself as president-elect to his consumable product line.

Deep into the presidential election season now, the mainstream news establishment's omnivorous 24-7 coverage of Trump has desensitized everyone. As a society, we have hit a media saturation point on the question of Trump's electability. Going forward, we shall likely feel and think nothing more from consuming *more* facts about Donald Trump, tuning it out as white noise rather than tuning it in as fodder for private epiphanies that guide voting preferences.

However, more compelling than understanding Donald Trump, the individual, is to understand the Trump Card he would brandish as American president. In card games, a trump card is elevated above normal rank cards. It has arbitrary, predetermined power that can override all other rules in the game. When a player uses the trump card, that player undertakes a potentially game-winning, game-ending move that *trumps* all other rules. If we elect Donald Trump as president, he will brandish such a Trump Card in the game of American politics. When played a president, the Trump Card can bend, suspend, or break any of the political or legal rules in the constitutional order that are otherwise intended to limit government or protect liberty.

The Trump Card is not about a multibillionaire that covets power, the next best thing to money. History is replete with them. The Trump Card is about strong man rule in a constitutional liberal democracy. It is about the de facto *carte blanche* of American constitutional government that results from entrusting an unpredictable president with the keys to a government office that wields unlimited, unaccountable power.

In this light, the Trump Card is a cast iron sword of Damocles hanging over the fate of our Constitution. If played by an American president in the ordinary course of constitutional politics, the Trump Card permits the American presidency to formulate and fund the administration of global, unilateral, secret, and selectively illiberal policies during the inter-election period. From drone warfare to dragnet surveillance, from perhaps building a U.S.-Mexico wall to banning Muslims, these executive policies are generally implemented without congressional authorization or judicial review before they start and without an iota of accountability after they end. This pattern in American constitutional politics has normalized since World War II, pretext by pretext, war by war, covert operation by covert operation, and administration by administration from Truman to Obama.

It is *this* government, *this* presidency, and *this* Trump Card, that Donald Trump may inherit on January 20th 2017. As is, Donald Trump's use of the Trump Card from the Oval Office would let him do what he wants, when he wants, however he wants, for virtually any reason he conjures, in secret or in plain view, and unencumbered by checks or balances during the execution of the policy and inoculated from accountability after the fact.

Just like a Roman dictator.

In this regard, the latest op-ed pieces on Trump's psychological unsuitability for the American presidency are seasonal and certainly inform and enlighten the private calculus of voter preferences as November 8th nears. At the same time, also salient in this private calculus is our general understanding of the grave, material risk that flows from entrusting the preponderant power and secrecy of the executive branch and presidency to an individual such as Donald Trump, who has brazenly proven over the course of the election campaign to be as racist as inexperienced, as obtuse as overconfident.

Art of Government

Recall how democratic government works.

In a pure Athenian democracy, the people ruled themselves. Political participation was direct and the community's social contract converted popular consent to political power directly, as illustrated in Figure 1.

Fig. 1: Consent-to-Power Flow

However, the modern American model is a bit different from the ancient Athenian one. We don't have a pure form of direct democracy. We have a *republican* framework of democratic government. That means we practice direct democracy *through* representative politics.

In our flavor of self-rule, we don't really rule ourselves directly. We rule ourselves by electing our representatives to formulate and effectuate policies on our behalf, during and in between the election cycles that periodically give us the opportunity to form a new government. In this way, the American social contract converts consent to governmental power to representative government policy, as illustrated in Figure 2.

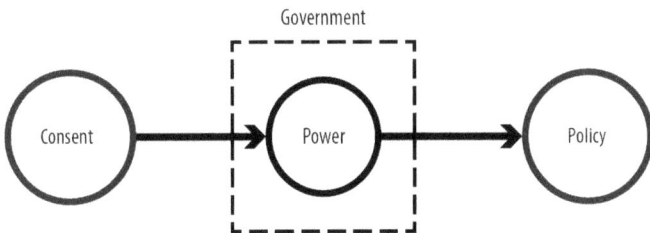

Fig. 2: Consent-to-Policy Flow

Here, the elected republic, headquartered in Washington, acts like a trusted middleman that translates the consent of the governed to representative government policies in real-time.

However, sometimes, middlemen don't behave like they are supposed to, especially when left unsupervised and shielded from scrutiny or accountability for breach of trust or loyalty.

In American politics, we have found this out the hard way. Even in democracies, elected governments – the middlemen between consent and policy – can abuse the power they wield by selectively devising and executing policies that may be non-representative, unlawful, or illiberal. It is at this nexus of consent and power where the Trump Card, and the clear and present danger it poses to the American constitutional order, is born. It is also at this nexus where the American presidency can wax imperial and the American president can look, walk, and talk like an elected dictator vis-à-vis certain policy domains like foreign affairs or national security.

Thus far, Trump's strong man appeal combines the worst of an elected president with the best of a draconian dictator. Trump's steady, unstoppable tromp to the center stage of American presidential politics reminds us of Cassius' colloquy with Brutus in Shakespeare's *Julius Caesar,* referring to the rise of the Roman dictator:

> Why, man, he doth bestrode the narrow world like a
> Colossus, and we petty men walk under his huge legs
> and peep about to find ourselves dishonorable graves.[2]

In certain respects, our two-party system has made American presidential politics a *narrow world*. In it, Trump has become a *Colossus* since July 19th.

Trump's meteoric rise has plunged the gilded, seemingly untouchable political establishment in Washington into anarchic tumult while unsettling elite camps on both sides of the aisle. Since Trump announced his presidential candidacy last year in New Hampshire on June 16th, 2015, a thickening thread of bipartisan befuddlement has cut through American public debate, from the *Washington Post* to the *New York Times*, CNN to the *Huffington Post*, the Associated Press to Al-Jazeera.

The democratic possibility of a President Trump has ineluctably evolved. In 2015, it was simply moronic, sort of like the absurd proposition of marijuana legalization in the 1990s. But times change in unpredictable ways. In 2016, a potential Trump presidency careens from a shot in the dark to shockingly plausible. The center of gravity of mainstream political discourse has followed suit.

Journalists used to bemusedly pontificate: "Is Donald Trump really running?" Now, the apprehension has shifted in scope and gravitas: "What happens if Donald Trump actually wins?"

A Hobson's Choice

A brash demagogue in the otherwise tediously choreographed and curated china shop of American presidential politics, Donald Trump at his best has exposed the American de facto superpower at her most vulnerable.

To be clear, the plight of the American voter in our two-party system is unenviable in the eyes of many. Our two choices in this presidential election are either Donald Trump or the Democratic Party's official nominee, Hillary R. Clinton. While many agree that Trump is vulnerable to attack for his character and inexperience, others would posit that Clinton is no paragon of virtue herself. Ironic, isn't it? The promise of democracy is about the people's choice. Yet, right here and now, while one camp supports Trump and another supports Clinton, a considerable segment of the electorate -- nearly one in four Americans -- dislikes both candidates.[3]

This segment can't vote for whom they like. Instead, they must cast ballots for the candidate they abhor less, a cruel Hobson's choice, like being forced to select between Scylla and Charybdis for a roommate, or being asked by your doctor if you prefer Herpes or Hepatitis B. If you actually had a choice, you might say, neither. Yet, here we are. Love it or hate it, this is our perfect Union's democratic process.

A significant point of distinction between a Trump presidency and Clinton presidency is the notion of *presidential risk*. If Trump's campaign foreshadows his administration, Trump simply presents unknown, unprecedented risks to American politic and global leadership that are amplified by the immense power attached to the American presidency. The risks that a Clinton presidency poses do exist, but within a normative spectrum. These are simply different in degree and kind from the risks presented by a Trump presidency.

He is inexperienced, untested, and psychologically volatile. She is the wife of former President Bill Clinton, the former Secretary of State of the Obama administration, and for better or worse, is a vetted, tried, tested, safer, and an electable presidential candidate who presents known, familiar risks.

Still, Trump, the multibillionaire, marches competitively onward, rebranding himself as a working class hero, a populist *deus ex machina* that promises to make America great again, the antidote for failed government. Lacking a coherent vision of substantive policy reform, Trump has ridden a wave of anti-establishment fervor fed by his tit-for-tat *ad hominem* attacks on opponents and journalists. Trump's outsider appeal has galvanized the trust of voters who distrust Washington politicians. Today, he is the straight talking human sponge for generalized rage, disillusionment, and Anglo-Saxon nativism. His tribal brand of racial neo-McCarthyism is calculated to systematically build his voting base by hyperbolic vilification of hypothetical external threats from Iran to ISIS, Muslims to Mexicans. Over the past year, this campaign platform has morphed into a well-oiled campaign machine that converts the fear of the governed into the consent of the governed.

Trump's mass appeal has spread virally too, to the dismay of liberal elites.

More, it has hardened in pockets of America's neglected, invisible white underclass that stretch from Mechanicsburg, Pennsylvania to Modoc County, California. To be sure, their grievances are legitimate and they now speak loudly in a *lingua franca* that Washington hears: presidential poll numbers.

From Truman to Obama, our national priorities have inexorably been inverted. A zero-sum game due to the finite nature of government resource allocations, the ascent of Washington's foreign affairs imperatives in American politics has demoted areas of domestic policy to secondary considerations. The global ripple effects are hidden in plain view. Today, we build schools in Kabul, not Detroit; we modernize security forces in Bogota, not Ferguson; we fight terrorism in

Yemen, not gun violence in our ghettos from New Orleans to Newark; our economy outsources work abroad more than it creates jobs at home. Post-1945 American hegemony has been built – brick by brick, policy by policy – on the spine of the government's structural neglect of this voiceless and invisible segment of the American citizenry that votes and pays taxes but see few meaningful changes to quality-of-life conditions in the zip codes where they reside. Trump has successfully tapped in to this volcanic reservoir of neglect, rage, and disillusionment to build out his voting base.

And as Trump continues to do so, the clock that counts down to November 8th ticks.

Glazed and aphasic, many of us watch in paralytic awe. Trump has made President Obama eat his roasting words from the 2011 White House correspondents' dinner. Trump has sent career politicians like Ted Cruz, Jeb Bush, and Marco Rubio packing, forcing them to 'suspend' their campaigns, submissively toe the party line by endorsement or silence, and watch the presidential elections from the bench. Just like us. Washington's creeping failure in representative government has finally spawned a monster it can't seem to tame or civilize. Now, we, the silent majority, brace for the presidential electoral outcome.

In hindsight, the writing was on the wall way back in February 2016. In his *Rolling Stone* article, *How America Made Donald Trump Unstoppable,* journalist Matt Taibi couldn't have summed up the unthinkable perfect storm of Trump's meteoric ascent any more succinctly:

> A thousand ridiculous accidents needed to happen in the unlikeliest of sequences for it to be possible, but absent a

dramatic turn of events – an early primary catastro-
phe, Mike Bloomberg ego-crashing the race, etc. – this
boorish, monosyllabic TV tyrant with the attention
span of an Xbox-playing 11-year-old really is set to lay
waste to the most impenetrable oligarchy the Western
world ever devised. It turns out we let our electoral process devolve into something so fake and dysfunctional
that any half-bright con man with the stones to try it
could walk right through the front door and tear it to
shreds on the first go. And Trump is no half-bright con
man, either. He's way better than average.[4]

Indeed, we might trace early warning signs of a Trump
presidential candidacy back even further to 2008 when John
McCain and Sarah Palin secured the Republican nomination
for president, or to 2012 when Mitt Romney did.

The hard truth is this: today, the Republican Party has
become desperately depleted of electable Presidential
talent. You might compare the contemporary GOP to a
lone Rolls Royce that is low on petrol on a flat country
road. Eventually, the vehicle will stop moving forward,
irrespective of how pretty the driver thinks it is or how
hard he pushes the pedal to the metal. And when the
Republican Party runs out of presidential petrol, what do
you get? The official Republican nomination of Donald
Trump for President of the United States, a black swan
candidate who may just trample over the American
constitutional order with untrammeled rapacity, from day
one in the Oval Office.

Sure, we can vote Trump in – that's what democracy is
all about. But, are the four corners of our Constitution

sufficient to tame and civilize his policies after we do, at home *and* abroad? Imagine. Just a few months away, in Q1 of 2017, a Trump administration might issue executive orders to ban Muslims, build a wall along the U.S.-Mexican border, commence deportation of 11 million undocumented immigrants, and greenlight the bombing of non-white families with alleged affiliation to U.S.-defined foreign terrorist organizations on foreign soil.

Is this the same America whose Civil Rights Revolution and Supreme Court produced pro-equality rulings like *Brown v. Board of Education*[5] in 1954?

What is happening in America?

What has happened to America *already*?

At the heart of this electoral quagmire is the most troubling riddle: will Donald Trump, a black swan presidential candidate, mutate into a Trojan horse as president-elect *after* election day, when our consent becomes de facto irrevocable until 2020? Is the Trump brand of rage-fueled demagogy poisonous to our social fabric? Does Trump's draconian vision to make America great again extol who we are or betray the social contract once fought for by the patriots who stained the white snows of Lexington and Concord dark red?

In the final analysis, is Donald Trump our Nation's savior or a clear and present danger to our system of constitutional government? We, the people, must decide by November 8th. The binary choice between red and blue has bruised the body politic purple.

Who are you voting for?

2

Trumpophobia

Trumpophobia *trəmp-ō-fō-bē-ə*\
(n.) the pathological fear, revulsion, loathing of the reasonable democratic possibility that we, the people, may
elect Donald Trump as President of the United States.

With the sobering benefit of inchoate hindsight, one
might argue that the GOP's official nomination of
Trump in July 2016 was as traumatically shocking to many
as Al Qaeda's 9/11 attacks were in September 2001.

We simply didn't see it coming, did we?

The sheer volume of print and digital news reporting
that has inundated front page headlines and smartphone
flat screens evidences the public mind's coping mechanism
from the trauma. Like 9/11, the GOP official nomination
of Trump shocked. It was personal and intangible, time-
bound yet transcendent, a big bang singularity in political
life with polymorphous butterfly effects that have touched
all strata of American society. It incited riots. It affected
families. It won't be forgotten. It *still* quickens the emo-
tional blood of the rational mind.

It also created a before and an after, making for a moment
in the national life of our republic that future historians

might one day say changed the trajectory of American constitutional politics. And like the effect of any traumatic exogenous shock, the GOP nomination makes us look in the mirror and question who we are as a Nation.

Today, Trump's electoral footprint is everywhere, all the time. He has dumbfounded the engaged citizen and politicized the apathetic, invigorated the nativist and anti-establishment rebel while delivering mortifying heart palpitations to the sacred breast of Washington's liberal elite. The Trump brand has obtained political omnipresence. From Starbucks cafes to Facebook, the subway to nail salons, bars to yoga studios, and dinner tables to the backseat of an Uber ride, the plumber, the policeman, the playwright, the porn star, the celebrity publicist, the pre-K teacher, the panhandler are all talking about Trump.

Trumpophobia has spread in the shadow of Trump's electoral footprint. As collateral damage, it has unraveled our electoral politics into a game of Russian roulette. Trumpophobia is the yin to the yang of Trumpism's growing mass appeal, silently burgeoning from a fleeting doubt in the minds of a few to an omnipresent public anxiety that continues to smother the presidential election season. From his vituperative tweetstorms to uncivilized public diatribes, stories about Trump routinely permeate the 24-7 digital news media cycle. Stories about Clinton are often no more than stories about her personification of a cure for Trumpophobia.

At its root, the singular focus of public discussion on Trump's electability is a symptom of a compound fear that has seized all walks of life, from President Obama[6] to *Washington Post* commentator Charles Krauthammer[7], from ex-C.I.A. director Michael J. Morell[8] to Supreme

Court justice Ruth B. Ginsberg[9], from rapper Young Jeezy[10] to Sen. Susan Collins[11] (R-ME).

Compound Fear

The compound fear of a Trump presidency is worth disentangling. Doing so helps us better understand *why* Trumpophobia has become an idée fixe that may actually start to shape anti-Trump voting choices on November 8th when our electoral process switches from statistical polling to ballot boxes.

Fundamentally, the compound fear of a Trump presidency has two aspects. The first aspect is personal. It is caused by the particular biography and psychological fitness of Donald Trump as an individual and his unfitness to serve as president in any democracy, let alone in America, a de facto superpower. The second aspect is structural. It is caused by our tacit acknowledgement of the omnipotence of the office that we, the people, may elect Donald Trump to occupy: the American presidency. Transformations of the American constitutional order since World War II have expanded the power of and weakened the constraints on the American presidency. In 21st century America, our American presidency possesses the power and autonomy to secretly pursue a set of illiberal policies at home and abroad that can range from torture to incommunicado detention, assassination by drone strike to dragnet surveillance.

These two aspects of the compound fear – Trump as individual and Trump as the president of a de facto superpower– are distinct but interrelated.

Recall that, American democracy is still hegemonic in the contemporary international system. America is still a de facto superpower. Granting a psychologically unfit individual such as Donald Trump unfettered access to immense concentrations of unlimited power that comes with the American presidency is a frightening proposition indeed. For instance, Trump's election sloganeering that has advocated for anti-Muslim and anti-Mexican policies is an ominous harbinger, seeming to endorse our Nation's return to the racially paranoid practices of our World War I-era days, animated by fear-laden group-think like the Yellow Peril or Red Scare.

Whether Trump is a misunderstood statesman or an unscrupulous mercantilist, Trump's neurotic quirks are just one aspect of Trumpophobia. An obsessive focus on this aspect distracts from the other aspect of Trumpophobia, namely the raw unchecked, unbalanced power we place in his hands if we elect him as President of the United States.

To be sure, the expanding scope of the American presidency's power within our constitutional order is not a recent development. It is the byproduct of a trifecta of trends in American constitutional politics that can be traced back to the Truman administration:

1. The concentration of power in a single branch of government, the executive branch, thereby weakening democratic controls on representative government;
2. The erosion of checks and balances within our political system to tame the executive branch in the policy domains of foreign affairs and national security;

3. The policy normalization of Washington's unaccountable global projection of unilateral power in secrecy without meaningful congressional authorization or judicial review.

These three trends form a mutually reinforcing cycle. First, power concentrates in the executive branch. Second, as it does, the checks and balances on the executive branch weaken to the point of non-existence vis-à-vis certain policy domains. Third, as they do, the executive branch normalizes the unchecked projection of unilateral power in these policy domains, such as foreign affairs and national security. Historically, this three-step process has repeated in a cycle.

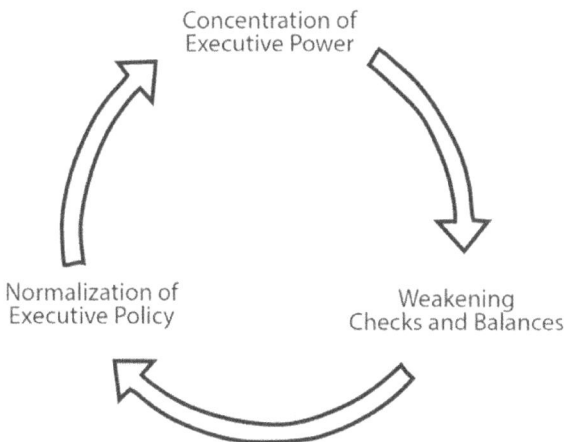

Fig. 3: Cycle of Power Concentration

As political power becomes more and more divorced from majoritarian consent, the process reconfigures a government once designed as a democracy to function as an ad hoc dictatorship as needs be, through its executive branch and presidency. Over time, Washington gets stronger as we, the people, get weaker. Indeed, we have seen this process repeat through transparent and secret waves of selectively illiberal policies that pervade almost a century of American statecraft, from the Bay of Pigs to Abu Ghraib to the Obama presidency's secret drone assassination of American citizen Samir Khan in Yemen in 2011 and beyond. Interestingly, the legality of this process, a taboo layer of contemporary American geopolitics, is backed by the optics of jurisprudence. In both courts of law and the American public square to this day, zealous advocates of an energetic executive branch in foreign affairs and national security have routinely invoked the landmark Supreme Court case *United States v. Curtiss-Wright Export Corp.*[12] *(1936),* a pre-World War II-era precedent. Justice Sutherland's majority opinion in *Curtiss-Wright* states in relevant part:

> It is important to bear in mind that we are here dealing not alone with an authority vested in the President by an exertion of legislative power, but with such an authority plus the very delicate, plenary and exclusive power of the President as the sole organ of the federal government in the field of international relations – a power which does not require as a basis for its exercise an act of Congress, but which of course, like every other governmental power, must be exercised in subordination to the applicable provisions of the Constitution.[13]

In other words, once elected, the American president can project American power as a benevolent dictator would.

The American president can do so by virtue of commanding the American presidency, a *sole organ* of government with *exclusive power* in the *field of international relations.* Contested but not overruled, the spirit of *Curtiss-Wright* has been a compass that has legitimized American power and guided American policy during the Cold War and the War on Terror.

The *Curtiss-Wright* vision of executive omnipotence starkly diverges from our republic's 1787 political blueprint. This vision *is* part of the 21st century American system of government. This vision *is* part of our rule of constitutional law. Frighteningly, this vision would probably be further extended by Donald Trump if we elect him as president.

A Poor Man's Lenin

Historical circumstance is a third factor that tacitly fans the flames of Trumpophobia from Silicon Valley to Soho as November 8th nears. In the broad brush of American national life, more and more, anti-establishment uprisings on the homeland like the Civil Rights revolution or Occupy Wall Street have become outliers as America has ascended to the apex of power in the international arena. Since 1945 in particular, by and large we simply have not confronted the tenacious rise of a demagogue with national appeal on the American presidential stage.

However, this phenomenon is not unprecedented in world affairs.

Consider the benevolent rise of Nelson Mandela in 1994 that displaced the dehumanizing chokehold of

Apartheid rule in white South Africa. On the other hand, consider the autocratic rise of Hugo Chavez in an oil-rich Venezuela whose clutch on democratic power included the simple *Chauvismo* formula of "exploiting inequality and social grievances to demonize the opposition."[14] In the public mind and in different ways, Mandela and Chavez converted anti-establishment animus to democratic hope. Such political conditions in Russia circa World War I also nurtured the revolutionary rise of Vladimir Lenin.

As it turns out, GOP presidential nominee Trump appears to be a poor man's Lenin. Thus far, Trump's election campaign strategy and mercurial policy platforms have eerily followed a Lenin-like playbook from 1917 that catapulted the political philosopher exiled in Switzerland to a communist leader of the Bolshevik Revolution.

Fig. 4: Viktor Deni's 1920 Bolshevik cartoon showing Lenin sweeping away monarchs, clergy, and capitalists.[15] [Russian Translation: Comrade Lenin cleans the Earth from impurities]

Тов. Ленин ОЧИЩАЕТ
землю от нечисти.

In 1917, the economic and political toll of war made times tough in Russia, and suffering and confusion rampant. British historian Eric Hobsbawm describes Lenin's playbook to rise to power through revolution under such conditions:

> Lenin's extraordinary achievement was to transform [the] uncontrollable anarchic popular surge into Bolshevik power ... The basic demand of the city poor was for bread ... The basic demand of the 80 per cent of Russians who lived by agriculture, was, as always, for land. Both agreed that they wanted an end to the war .. These slogans, 'Bread, Peace, Land' won rapidly growing support for those who propagated them, notably Lenin's Bolsheviks, who grew from a small troop of a few thousands in March 1917 to a quarter of a million members, by the early summer of that year. Contrary to the Cold War mythology, which saw Lenin essentially as an organizer of coups, the only real asset he and the Bolsheviks had was the ability to recognize what the masses wanted; to, as it were, *lead by knowing how to follow.* (italics added)

Echoing Hobsbawm, Edward Crankshaw, another historian, remarks similarly of Lenin's rise in 1917:

> In the suffering and confusion of revolutionary Russia [Lenin] held aloof from those who were trying to make the revolution work ... He appealed to the people, the soldiers, the workers, the peasants ... He appealed to their most selfish instincts: the desire for bread, for land, for peace.

And, in the end, he got them on his side sufficiently to overthrow the government of Petrograd.[16]

Perspicaciously, like Trump now in the American context, Lenin made himself a human sponge for popular grievances by mobilizing on a revolutionary platform that would resonate throughout Russia: Bread, Peace, and Land! Lenin led by giving the people what he believed they wanted. As Hobsbawm notes, Lenin led by *knowing how to follow.*

Trump has led by learning how to follow too, retrofitting the policy platforms of his presidential campaign to appeal to the xenophobic and nativist instincts that are ingrained in his mind and that he sensed were latent in broad segments of American society. Instead of Lenin's Bread, Peace, and Land slogan or Lenin's promise to sweep away the Russian monarchs, clergy, and capitalists, Trumpism mobilizes political support around three pillars: building a U.S.-Mexico wall, banning Muslims, and deporting millions of undocumented immigrants. Like Lenin, Trump too, it seems has learned to *lead by learning how to follow.*

To be clear, Donald Trump is not a politician. He is a mercantilist with *only* presidential aspirations. Donald Trump has not spent his life in politics like Mandela, Chavez, and Lenin did, or like many mayors or senators in American politics have. To compensate for political inexperience, what Trump does have is the preternatural timing of a multibillionaire real estate mogul. In business, he knows when to invest. In presidential elections, it appears, for all he lacks, he certainly knew when to run.

Anti-Trump Counterrevolution

Trumpophobia is real. It forces us to look candidly in the mirror at who we are and what our government has become, even if only for a fleeting moment.

In this regard, time is precious. Trumpophobia is a fleeting spotlight. If we open our eyes, Trumpophobia illuminates how the American nation-state has radically changed in form and function since 9/11, 1989, 1945, or 1787 even. On balance, Trumpophobia is an ironic blessing for American politics as well, one that has invigorated and united the body politic as much as Trumpism has polarized and divided it.

For the better, the enlightening epidemic of Trumpophobia has tested our Nation's common purpose and moral character, building pluralistic consensus through anti-Trump resistance as much as it has broken multicultural social bonds through fear and hate. In fact, on varying grounds, several prominent American voices from different stripes of political life have joined an increasingly universal Trumpophobic chorus as November 8th nears. While the numbers infected with Trumpophobia have grown significantly from patient zero since summer of 2015, consider the following four voices as illustrative of the fledgling anti-Trump counter-revolution.

First, David Brooks of the *New York Times* discusses Trump's mental instability in his article, *Trump is getting even Trumpier*, published on July 19th:

> *This is a unique moment in American political history in which the mental stability of one of the major party nominees is the dominating subject of conversation* ... The structure of

his mental perambulations also seems to have changed. Formerly, as I said, his speeches had a random, free-form quality. But on Saturday his remarks had a distinct through line, anchored by the talking points his campaign had written down on pieces of paper. But Trump could not keep his attention focused on this through line — since the subject was someone else — so every 30 seconds or so he would shoot off on a resent-ment-filled bragging loop … Suddenly the global climate favors a Trump candidacy. Some forms of dis-order — like a financial crisis — send voters for the calm supple thinker. But other forms of disorder — blood in the streets — send them scurrying for the brutal strongman. If the string of horrific events continues, Trump could win the presidency. And he could win it even though he has less and less control over himself.[17] (italics added)

Second, George F. Will of the *Washington Post* dissects the G.O.P's acquiescence in the duplicity of Trump and Pence in his article, Trumps Shallowness Runs Deep, published on August 4th:

The nation, however, is not immune to the lasting damage that is being done to it by Trump's success in normalizing post-factual politics. It is being poisoned by the injection into its bloodstream of the cynicism required of those Republicans who persist in pretending that although Trump lies constantly and knows nothing, these blem-ishes do not disqualify him from being president … Pence, doing his well-practiced imitation of a country vicar saddened by the discovery of sin in his parish, said with sorrowful solemnity: "I don't think name-calling has any place in public life." As in "Lyin' Ted" Cruz and "Little Marco" Rubio and "Crooked Hillary" Clinton?[18] (italics added)

Third, Charles Krauthammer of the *Washington Post* analyzes whether Trump's neurotic quirks undermine is presidential electability in his article, *Donald Trump and the Fitness Threshold*, published on August 4th:

Trump's hypersensitivity and unedited, untempered Pavlovian responses are, shall we say, unusual in both ferocity and predictability ... *This is beyond narcissism. I used to think Trump was an 11-year-old, an undeveloped schoolyard bully. I was off by about 10 years.* His needs are more primitive, an infantile hunger for approval and praise, a craving that can never be satisfied. He lives in a cocoon of solipsism where the world outside himself has value — indeed exists — only insofar as it sustains and inflates him ... Trump's greatest success — normalizing the abnormal — is beginning to dissipate. When a Pulitzer Prize-winning liberal columnist (Eugene Robinson) and a major conservative foreign policy thinker and former speechwriter for George Shultz under Ronald Reagan (Robert Kagan) simultaneously question Trump's psychological stability, indeed sanity, there's something going on (as Trump would say).[19] (italics added)

Krauthammer continues, comparing this election to Ronald Reagan's in 1980.

The dynamic of this election is obvious. As in 1980, the status quo candidate for a failed administration is running against an outsider. The stay-the-course candidate plays his/her only available card — charging that the outsider is dangerously out of the mainstream and temperamentally unfit to command the nation ... In 1980, Reagan had to do just one thing: pass the threshold test for acceptability. He won that election because he did, especially in the debate with Jimmy Carter in which Reagan showed himself to be genial, self-assured and, above all, nonthreatening. You may not like all his policies, but you could safely entrust the nation to him. Trump badly needs to pass that threshold. If character is destiny, he won't.[20]

And lastly, ex-CIA director Michael J. Morell describes the risks a Trump presidency would present to American national security in his *New York Times* article, *I ran the C.I.A. Now I'm Endorsing Hillary Clinton*, published on August 5th:

During a 33-year career at the Central Intelligence Agency, I served presidents of both parties — three Republicans and three Democrats. I was at President George W. Bush's side when we were attacked on Sept. 11; as deputy director of the agency, I was with President Obama when we killed Osama bin Laden in 2011 ... As a government official, I have always been silent about my preference for president ... No longer. On Nov. 8, I will vote for Hillary Clinton. Between now and then, I will do everything I can to ensure that she is elected as our 45th president ... *[T]he dangers that flow from Mr. Trump's character are not just risks that would emerge if he became president. It is already damaging our national security.*[21] *(italics added)*

If we can see past Trump the individual and through the fog of Trumpism, Trumpophobia is about our constitutional government's absence of meaningful checks and balances on the presidency. It has forced us to confront the notion that an energetic executive in our system of constitutional government *can* moonlight as a double-edged sword when placed in unwise hands through democratic means or otherwise, slaying our enemies, but tearing our social contract asunder in the process. If the post-9/11 administrations of mainstream GOP and Democratic Party presidents like George W. Bush or Barack Obama were capable of secret illiberal policies like torture and drone warfare from Cuba to Somalia, what is a Trump administration capable of? As is, what checks and balances can our system of constitutional government place in Trump's path if elected?

James Madison aptly surmised this conundrum in *Federalist No. 51*,

[i]n framing a government which is to be administered by men over men, the great difficulty lies in this: you must first enable the government to control the governed; and in the next place, oblige it to control itself.[22]

Could our constitutional democracy tame or civilize a Trump presidency? Will Trump embrace a politics of self-restraint or elective despotism as president? These are open questions, ones that present unknown, potentially catastrophic risks to American government at home and American global leadership abroad.

For all that remains unknown about the risks that a Trump presidency would present to the Nation, what we can say with a reasonable degree of certainty now is that the basic form and function of American government has changed radically since 1787. The raw power of the modern American presidency has outstripped the 18th century design constraints intended to check and balance against it within our system of constitutional government. Indeed, a century of American statecraft evidences this structural transformation. The Truman administration sent troops to Korea in 1954 without congressional authorization. The Obama administration conducted a post-9/11 global counterterrorism program that included dragnet surveillance and targeted assassination by drone strike that included American citizens, all without congressional authorization or judicial review. The non-impeachments of Nixon or George W. Bush for grave, material breaches of international humanitarian and human rights law during the Cold War and War on Terror are gross omissions in presidential accountability that set ominous precedents for the future aggrandizement and non-accountability of executive policy within the American constitutional order.

Odd as it may seem, Nixon and Bush are quite tame and civilized in comparison to Trump. However, it is all relative, isn't it? Human cannibal Jeffrey Dahmer might seem like a tame, civilized dinner date if your alternative is a very hungry Tyrannosaurus Rex.

The obvious, persistent concern with a Trump presidency

is that the limits of American exceptionalism are unknown if they exist at all. Accordingly, we simply don't know what could happen if the unlimited, unaccountable power of the American presidency were to be democratically transferred to the unwise hands of a multibillionaire accustomed to dividing and conquering the real estate market. If a Truman or Obama are capable of policies of needlessly putting our troops in harms way or torturing non-white enemy combatant suspects in a fishing expedition to extract actionable intelligence, what degree of self-restraint should we reasonably expect from Donald Trump?

As humans, we habituate. We have no Archimedean point to see our own lives with a fresh lens of clarity, an intransigent blind spot that makes it easy for us to lose sight of the simple things sometimes. In the upcoming election of America's 45th president, one might be this: America is not Luxembourg or Bangladesh.

We're still a superpower in many ways. Our presidential election is the world's most important one because our democracy is the world's most powerful one, a de facto hegemon without a peer in today's increasingly post-superpower multipolarizing world. It is true that China and Russia along with other regional powers have grown economically and politically stronger than they were at the end of the Cold War when the Berlin Wall fell. Such shifts have relatively diminished American full-spectrum dominance in the field of international relations. Be that as it may, we still project power globally. We still have military bases all around the world. We still maintain a global sphere of national interest whose mix of positive and malevolent butterfly effects ripple outward from Washington.

To this day, public and secret decisions made in the White House and Capital Hill by our elected or appointed officials tweak, touch, tame, twist, and torment the everyday politics of every nation-state in the international system from Sao Paulo to Shanghai, Moscow to Havana.

Contemporary Washington is not like Caesar's Rome. It is our republic's headquarters, not an empire's throne. That said, Washington inarguably wields immense and historically unprecedented concentrations of power that have fueled secret, illiberal global policies, from torture in Cuba to drone strikes in Yemen to extraordinary rendition from Somalia to Afghanistan.

All said and done, that's a lot of power, unilateralism, secrecy, and selective unaccountability, even if modern American government had functional checks and balances.

Come January 20th, 2017, all of it may be placed in the hands of Donald Trump, the aspiring philosopher-king who seems to be *all* king in his heart and *no* philosophy between his ears. Should we entrust this omnipotent Leviathan-esque American presidency in his hands?

If our nationalistic sentiments sway us, we must remind ourselves that while patriotic fidelity is virtuous, mindless patriotism is an opiate that is anathema to intelligent self-government. If bipartisan groupthink and our individualistic party allegiance blind us, an analogous question tests the same principle of decision at this troubled nexus of democratic choice and political power.

Republican or Democrat, would you trust an irascible teenager with a surface-to-air rocket launcher?

You might think twice before doing so. Maybe we should as well on November 8th.

3

Roman Dictator Cincinnatus

dictator *dik-tā-tər*\
(n.) a person who rules a country with total authority and often in a cruel or brutal way.[23]

Has the American presidency become so strong it waxes imperial during crises? When executive power is concentrated and preponderant and executive policy is at its most secret and unaccountable, does the American president begin to look, walk, and talk like an elected dictator during certain political moments, more or less?

At first impression, this hypothetical scenario pricks the American public consciousness as a ludicrous, logical *non sequitor*. How could it ever be so, we say? America is a constitutional liberal democracy, not an empire or dictatorship. *How can the modern American presidency possess the unaccountable, illimitable power of an empire or dictatorship when we elect our president and the institution of the presidency is constrained by the checks and balances of our system of government and rule of constitutional law?*

In theory, it can't.

In practice, however, the American presidency has proven time and again that it can flex ad hoc imperial, dictatorial powers in the policy domains of national security and foreign affairs. Over the past century, Washington's ad hoc flexing has crystallized into a pattern of American statecraft that encompasses the Cold War and War on Terror. Its regularity makes it as normative as unremarkable. The reason for this pertains to government structure. Washington's 21st century power has outstripped America's 18th century constitutional design. In our governmental structure, the *checks and balances* once designed by the Framers in 1787 no longer effectively check or balance against our modern executive branch that is headquartered in Washington today. Indeed, the government designs of 18th century America and of 21st century America have diverged substantially. If compared, the two designs are arguably unrecognizable now. To understand what checks and balances exist today, it is instructive to start with redefining what the design of modern American government actually is.

At present, we conceive our social contract as establishing one rule of law for one government. This is accurate. It is also reductive and entrenches popular misconceptions about how contemporary Washington works in practice.

American government design is hybrid. America is a democracy. America is *also* a republic. America is a democracy *and* a republic under one rule of constitutional law. The terms democracy and republic are erroneously used almost synonymously in mainstream political commentary. They are not synonymous. A democracy and a republic are distinct paradigms of political rule with dissimilar social contracts. *In democracy, the people rule themselves.* From its Greek root, *demokratia*, the word "democracy" means rule (*kratos*) by the people (*demos*). *In a republic, the few rule the many.* From its Latin root, *res publica*, the word "republic" originated from the meaning, an entity (*res*) of the people (*publicus*), and has come to mean an elected governing body that rules a political society.

Modern America is not one or the other. She is both in the same breath – a *democracy-republic chimera.*

Pursuant to this hybrid social contract that harmonizes democratic and republican features in one system of constitutional government, *the many periodically elect the few to rule the people, ad infinitum.* This is how Washington works. It was true in 1776. It is still true today. While our democracy-republic chimera has been extolled for its infallible genius in the dusty liberal canons of Western political and constitutional theory, this blended design of the government we have – that is part democracy, part republic – can produce dysfunctional, non-representative policies too.

Think the Bay of Pigs or Abu Ghraib. Think the Iran-Contra Affair and Watergate or drone warfare and dragnet surveillance. Think COINTELPRO and arming murderous paramilitaries in Guatemala and El Salvador during the Cold War, force-feeding hunger striker detainees in the War on Terror, or the CIA's shackling, torture, and blunt instrument sodomy of German citizen Khaled El-Masri, in a fetid, secret CIA-run black site prison in Afghanistan after his extraordinary rendition from Macedonia. From Truman to Obama, historical examples are innumerable. They make for a long, running, sordid laundry list of America's selectively illiberal policies since 1945, democratized by the American voter and bankrolled by American taxpayer.

Here, our democratic consent that should guarantee that government policies remain representative in the inter-election period is politically powerless. Even though we live in a democratic society, our consent in such situations has virtually no influence on the formulation and administration of such secret and allegedly representative government policies, generally morally indefensible in the public square. Our voice is further weakened and muzzled by the implicit bipartisan consensus that sustains these policies. If both parties -- Democrat and Republican – tacitly support using torture in interrogations, what political recourse does the American citizen have in such two party system? You can't vote that policy out of government, can you? In this moment, absent populist revolution in the public square, the people have no democratic remedy to correct Washington's non-representative policies.

In such moments, the democratic force of the American presidential ballot is politically bankrupt. It has zero value. The resulting feeling of political powerlessness is not unfamiliar. The spirit of liberty that such political powerlessness suffocates typically fights back if it can, sparking anti-war demonstrations during Vietnam and public-interest whistleblowing after 9/11. But sometimes the force of liberty is insufficient and powerlessness prevails, even in American society, the land of the free and home of the brave.

There is a common domestic political thread connecting such historical moments like the American wars in Vietnam or Afghanistan: *Washington waxes omnipotent and we, the people, wax powerless.* The American presidency, headquartered in Washington, is well aware of this constitutional imbalance in unchecked executive power, and naturally, offers no objection. If blow came to blow, the American presidency has learned that it can ultimately trump or circumnavigate democratic counter-forces that might impede a plan to effectuate non-representative policies. Additionally, despite the past century of American selective illiberalism in foreign affairs and national security, we have seen only two presidential impeachments under Art. II of the Constitution since 1787. One of the presidential impeachments was initiated in 1998 against our then sitting 42nd President Bill Clinton on the grounds of perjury and obstruction of justice in connection with the salacious Monica Lewinsky scandal. The other impeachment occurred 130 years earlier in 1868 against then sitting President Andrew Jackson on multiple grounds including high crimes and misdemeanors.

That's it.

Nothing for Nixon and his involvement in the Watergate scandal or head-of-state responsibility for overseeing brutal anti-communism policies in Southeast Asia. Nothing for Bush II after 9/11 and his involvement in global counter-terrorism policies that have been widely acknowledged to have violated international humanitarian and human rights law. For that matter, nothing for any American wartime president from Woodrow Wilson in World War I to Barack Obama in the post-bin Laden War on Terror.

The modern American presidency has learned its lesson. Our constitutional republic demonstrates post-presidential impeachability. Due to persistent non-use, presidential impeachment is no longer a relevant legal threat to or constraint on the American presidency. More, no meaningful structural check or balance from the legislature or judiciary exists within our current system of constitutional government to stop the American presidency *in flagrante delicto* or punish it after for illiberal or unlawful policies it may deem as necessary to protect the national interest.

Thomas Jefferson once wrote, "an elective despotism is not the government we fought for." And yet, it seems that is exactly what we, the people, have experienced for almost a century during times of emergency. Any democracy waxes despotic when its executive branch usurps power without limit and exercises it without principled regulation. When the executive branch behaves in this manner, the executive branch and the presidency begin to walk, talk, look, feel, and function, like an ad hoc dictatorship. Here, our ballot still forms the government but can't control the government in the inter-election period in certain policy domains, like foreign affairs or national security.

This is problematic.

This is also the root cause of Trumpophobia and the paramount risk presented by a Trump presidency. By making Trump president, we invariably entrust this powerful institutional politico-military machinery – arguably the most powerful in the contemporary international system or for a democracy *ever* – to a Trump administration come January 20th 2017.

The Legend of Cincinnatus

Fig. 5: Roman Dictator Lucius Quinctius Cincinnatus

> *Trust the president, trust the executive branch.*
> *Trust the president, trust the executive branch.*

Close your eyes and repeat this Orwellian mantra.

Indeed, it seems like we, the people have been doing so since World War II, at least subconsciously. Repetition indoctrinates. In the human mind, public or individual, repetition can convert ideas into beliefs, beliefs into policies, policies into statecraft, and statecraft into norms of contemporary international relations. Since 1945, 'trust the president, trust the executive branch' has become the unstated mantra of American constitutional politics in the policy domains of national security and foreign affairs. This unstated mantra reflects a cardinal transformation in the structure of our political system, namely the gradual growth of the executive branch.

Our government is divided into three branches – the legislature, the executive, and the judiciary – that correspond to Art. I, II, and III of the Constitution. This constitutional doctrine of separation of powers sets up our government's system of checks and balances. However, the separation boundary is often more of an osmotic membrane than an Iron Curtain. This fluidity of the branches is intended to let our government function more like three chambers of one heart than three silos in a vacuum. When Congress is acquiescent and the judiciary spectates from the sidelines or merely rubber stamps government policy, the only branch active in our system of government is the executive branch.

Empowered to act alone, in the wake of the Cold War and over a decade into the post-9/11 War on Terror, our executive branch has essentially *done the work* that a strong man would do in a Developing World illiberal democracy or military dictatorship. The energy of our executive branch is legitimized as constitutional, and often functions like historical strong men such as a Mussolini, Pinochet, Pol Pot, or Rajapakse would, except on good, liberal behavior, deploying its unchecked powers in morally justifiable policy agendas that advance the national interest and international public good while keeping the Nation safe.

As democratic citizens, we convulse at the thought of our tax dollars and ballots supporting a *constitutional* elective dictatorship, a draconian bête noire administered by faceless bureaucrats in Washington. On its face, dictatorships are anti-democratic. The spirit of democracy runs through our blood, and accordingly, our reflex to dismiss comparisons of democracy to dictatorship is natural and reasonable.

However, Athenian citizens of ancient Rome, the cradle of Western political philosophy, would not have convulsed at hearing dictatorship and democracy in the same breath. To the contrary, they would have rejoiced. We believe democracy is good and dictatorship is bad. Athenians of ancient Rome believed that democracy is good and dictatorship is sometimes necessary.

In ancient times, Athenians once felt that integrating an ad hoc dictatorship option into the social contract of a republic was forward-thinking, efficient, and essential to the survival and safety of the republic. In the Athenian view, if ad hoc dictatorship posed an evil to good government, it posed a necessary evil. Sometimes, all the bureaucratic, deliberative decision-making of democratic politics slows you down. Sometimes you need to be agile and act quickly with decisive force. A dictatorship permits that. As such, the social contract of ancient Rome's republican government did not extirpate a place for a Roman dictator in times of emergency.

We all know of Julius Caesar, the Roman dictator whose thirst for military conquest transformed the Roman Republic into the Roman Empire, a fateful path that precipitated the ruin of republic and his own assassination. Less known is a more relevant Roman historical figure to contemporary American constitutional politics: Roman dictator Lucius Quinctius Cincinnatus.

Who was Cincinnatus?

Cincinnatus was the quintessential benevolent dictator. The legend of Cincinnatus in many ways legitimizes the institutions of America's energetic executive branch and imperial presidency within our constitutional order today. As the legend of Cincinnatus goes, Cincinnatus was a farmer who the Roman Senate appointed as Rome's dictator for sixteen days in 458 B.C. While post-9/11 America fights enemies of the state such as transnational non-state terrorist organizations, in 458 B.C., the Roman republic was fighting its own enemies of the republic, analogous to an Al Qaeda or ISIS in modern times: the Aequi and the Sabines. One day, an Aequian military offensive trapped the Roman army and Rome's consul in the Alban Hills. A few Roman horsemen who had escaped the military confrontation returned to Rome from the battlefield to inform the Senate. Roman national security was under threat. The Senate panicked. The Senate appointed Horatius Pulvillus as new consul, and subsequently ordered Horatius to appoint a dictator. Horatius selected Cincinnatus to temporarily rule Rome as dictator. When Cincinnatus was appointed dictator to respond to the Roman national security threat, Rome's political structure transformed from republic to dictatorship. Although Cincinnatus was entitled to legitimately remain Rome's dictator for six months under Roman law, Cincinnatus only held the title for only sixteen days during which he lead the Romans to military victory in the battle of Mons Algidus. After the battle was won, Cincinnatus disbanded the army, resigned as dictator, returned to his farm, and returned Rome to a republic.

While Caesar demonstrated the destruction a Roman dictator could inflict in the course of politics, Cincinnatus' brief rule as a dictator demonstrated the advantages of designing a republic to turn into an ad hoc dictatorship during a crisis if needs be.

To be clear, Cincinnatus was the anti-Caesar because although he had total authority over the Roman republic, he relinquished that power according to law. Cincinnatus', dictatorial rule was virtuous because it was temporary and renounced after the crisis dissipated. After appointment, Cincinnatus did not conspire to expand or attenuate his grip on power as dictator. He did the opposite. Cincinnatus returned Rome from an ad hoc dictatorship to a republic after military victory by relinquishing his dictatorial powers.

The Roman republic's and citizenry's implied trust in Cincinnatus to wield fleeting yet absolute power during war to protect Rome resonates, at least structurally, in the contemporary age with the imperial role of the American presidency and aggrandizement of executive power within the American constitutional order since 1945.

Since the days of Cincinnatus and Caesar, the Western definition of dictator has changed over the years, the evolutionary linguistic toll of the historical carnage and savagery exhibited by the early 20th century dictatorships of living memory, like those of Mussolini and Franco, Peron and Pol Pot. The past affects what vocabulary means in the future. To this extent, the modern definition of dictator is pernicious, stigmatized by the legacies of historical dictatorships from Caesar to Mussolini.

While Caesar's legacy is still demonized, the legend of Cincinnatus as a benevolent dictator lives on, arguably through the post-1945 role of an energetic executive in the American constitutional order. After 9/11, Bush was a

Caesar to some voters and a Cincinnatus to others. The same could be said of Obama, especially given the propensity of his administration to use executive orders and unadjudicated Art. II Commander-in-Chief powers to circumvent the checks and balances of our system of constitutional government.

Since Trump began campaigning in 2015, all evidence suggests that Trump would likely become a president who aspires to mimic the methods of Caesar, hardwired to hubristically covet more absolute power rather than less. To be sure, these are good instincts for a multibillionaire real estate mogul. These are not good instincts for a democratically elected president of a de facto superpower.

Early Philosophers

The notion of justifying a form of government that includes a dictatorial institution that can function like Cincinnatus did in the battle of Mons Algidus – without check and with unlimited power – is not new. Indeed it pervades Western political philosophy, and has been reiterated time and again by influential thinkers such as Machiavelli, Hamilton, and Lincoln. Each saw an energetic executive and benevolent dictatorship as a distinction without a difference in the crucible of crisis. Each would have defended and praised the ability of America's Union to adapt its anatomy to the exigencies of our age, and concentrate power in a single branch to keep the Nation safe.

In this regard, certain aspects of Western political culture haven't really changed since the 16th century. In government design, we still believe in the maxim that security is liberty's precondition. Without security, liberty dies. This philosophy of governance straddles millennia, from 16th century Italian monarchies to post-9/11 America. The design solution for government to keep their citizenries safe has always been some variation of a strong man, be it in human form like Cincinnatus or institutional form through an energetic executive branch or imperial presidency. To illustrate the common thread that connects the past of the West to a plausible future scenario in which Donald Trump might become the 45th American president, consider the writings of four eras: Niccolo Machiavelli in the 16th century, Hamilton in the 18th century, President Lincoln in the 19th century, and 20th century assertions of American policy in foreign affairs and national security during the embryonic stages of the Cold War.

Niccolo Machiavelli

While associated with his work, *The Prince,* which was written to advise princes on how to consolidate power and control populations within their kingdoms, Machiavelli elaborated upon the advantages of incorporating the ad hoc dictatorship option within the design of the Roman republic in *Discourses on Livy*, published in 1531. In *Discourses*, Machiavelli concluded that the Roman republic should maintain a dictatorship option to efficiently respond to crises with unfettered power because Rome's national security interest trumped the potential unpopularity of such concentrations of power. In *Discourse 34,* Machiavelli stated that,

[d]ictatorial [a]uthority did good, not harm, to the republic of Rome ... [and] it [wa]s the authority which
Citizens arrogate to Themselves, not that granted by
Free Suffrage, that [wa]s harmful to Civic Life ... Those
Romans who were responsible for the institution of a
dictatorship in Rome are condemned by some Roman
writers who find in the dictatorship the cause which
eventually led to tyranny in Rome.[24]

Machiavelli also spoke of Rome's accountable ad hoc
dictatorship. "It is clear," Machiavelli wrote,

that the dictatorship, so long as it was bestowed in accord-
ance with public institutions, and not assumed by the
dictator on his own authority, was always of benefit to the
state ... A dictator was appointed for a limited time, and for
the purpose of dealing solely with such matters as had led
to the appointment ... Wherefore, in view of the short
duration of the dictatorship, of the limited authority which
the dictator possessed, and of the fact that the Roman
people were not corrupt, it was impossible for the dictator
to overstep his terms of references and to do the state
harm ... Among all the other Roman institutions, [the dictatorship] truly deserves to be considered and numbered
among those which were the source of the greatness of
such an empire, because without a similar system cities
survive extraordinary circumstances only with difficulty.[25]

Machiavelli also believed that the ability of the republic to
transform to a dictatorship during crisis was vital to
Roman power and security because:

[t]he usual institutions in republics are slow to move . . . and, since time is wasted in coming to an agreement, the remedies for republics are very dangerous when they must find one for a problem that cannot wait.[26]

Machiavelli further believed as well that dictatorships are more efficient than republics because a small decision-making elite was better suited to respond to crisis:

Republics must therefore have among their laws a procedure . . . [that] reserve[s] to a small number of citizens the authority to deliberate on matters of urgent need without consulting anyone else, if they are in complete agreement. When a republic lacks such a procedure, it must necessarily come to ruin.[27]

Alexander Hamilton

A few centuries later, Alexander Hamilton, a Founding Father, echoed Machiavelli's pro-dictatorship views. In the 18th century, Hamilton made Machiavelli's argument in principle, advocating for a muscular, robust, "energetic," and quasi-autarkic Executive Branch to respond to crisis. In *Federalist No. 70*, referencing ancient Rome's structural ability to mutate from republic to dictatorship as the exigencies of Roman security required, Hamilton invokes Rome's republic-dictatorship chimera as worthy of emulation. "Energy in the Executive," Hamilton writes,

is a leading character in the definition of good government. It is essential to the protection of the community against foreign attacks; it is not less essential to the steady administration of the laws; to the protection of property against those irregular and high-handed combinations which sometimes interrupt the ordinary course of justice; to the security of liberty against the enterprises and assaults of ambition, of faction, and of anarchy. Every man the least conversant in Roman story, knows how often that republic was obliged to take refuge in the absolute power of a single man, under the formidable title of Dictator, as well against the intrigues of ambitious individuals who aspired to the tyranny, and the seditions of whole classes of the community whose conduct threatened the existence of all government, as against the invasions of external enemies who menaced the conquest and destruction of Rome.[28]

The Hamiltonian conception of an energetic Executive within the constitutional paradigm of American government does not go so far as to endorse American dictatorship. But, it does encourage the political accommodation of dictatorial qualities in a democracy while balancing the competing interests of maintaining republican virtues, as Rome did. The two models of political order – Machiavelli's republic and Hamilton's democracy - adapt their social contracts to permit the concentration of "power in a single hand" during crisis. Hamilton elaborates further on the energetic executive's desirable dictatorial attributes:

The ingredients which constitute energy in the Executive are, first, unity; secondly, duration; thirdly, an adequate provision for its support; fourthly, competent powers. The ingredients which constitute safety in the republican sense are, first, a due dependence on the people, secondly, a due responsibility ... That unity is conducive to energy will not be disputed. Decision, activity, secrecy, and dispatch will generally characterize the proceedings of one man in a much more eminent degree than the proceedings of any greater number; and in proportion as the number is increased, these qualities will be diminished.[29]

Abraham Lincoln

Thirdly, president Abraham Lincoln supported the incorporation of dictatorial qualities in democratic government, just like Machiavelli and Hamilton did. In Lincoln's time, the Northern abolition movement expedited the end of slavery. Violent secessionist impulses awakened in the South from the slow dismantling of the legal order that sustained the slave economy combined with the regional experience of political subjugation under the Union's new sovereign authority over the several states. The aggregate impact of these twin developments that strengthened the Union while threatening the way of life in the South lit a spark that ignited nation-wide instability in America's post-Revolution political order.

The American Civil War erupted, threatening the Union with the prospect of dissolution during Lincoln's Presidency. The crisis compelled Lincoln to redraw the balance between liberty and security within America's constitutional order so his administration could protect and preserve the Union, for instance taking various measures such as suspending the writ of habeas corpus. Echoing the legend of Cincinnatus, political philosophies of Machiavelli and Hamilton, Lincoln chose force over law, benevolently in Lincoln's mind. The threat posed to the Union by the Civil war "forces us to ask," Lincoln said,

> [i]s there, in all republics, this inherent and fatal weakness? Must a government, of necessity, be too strong for the liberties of its own people, or too weak to maintain its own existence?[30]

Lincoln did not expressly endorse dictatorship. He did endorse Rome's political structure. In Lincoln's view, dictatorial powers within the American political system could be generated by temporarily de-linking the exercise of government from the constraints of law during the bubble of crisis. Moreover, if the fate of the Nation hung in the balance, force – not law – was the weapon the state should rely upon for survival. Lincoln continues;

> The law is made for the state, not the state for the law ... If the circumstances are such that a choice must be made between the two, it is the law which must be sacrificed for the state. *Salus populi suprema lex esto*.[31]

Lincoln continues:

> Every man thinks he has a right to live and every government thinks it has a right to live. Every man when driven to the wall by a murderous assailant will override

all laws to protect himself, and this is called the great right of self-defense. So every government, when driven to the wall by a rebellion, will trample down a constitution before it will allow itself to be destroyed. This may or may not be constitutional law, but it is fact.[32]

The political thought of Machiavelli, Hamilton, Madison, and Lincoln that justifies concentrated executive power during times of emergency gives homage to the legend of Cincinnatus. Each of them viewed the Roman dictator as not only a celebrated creature of ancient Roman politics but a necessary paradigm for effective self-government. In the institutional form of an energetic executive and imperial presidency, the Roman dictator of the Cincinnatus variety has insidiously found a place in the American constitutional order.

Their thinking still reverberates today. During times of emergency, the American president is deemed omnipotent like a Roman dictator was. Consider the following view of presidential war powers asserted by the Bush administration after 9/11:

Irrespective of any Congressional assent, the President has broad powers as Commander in Chief of the Armed Forces under the Constitution that would justify the use of force in Iraq ... The Constitution vests the President with full "executive Power," and designates him "Commander in Chief" of the Armed Forces. Together, these provisions are a substantive grant of broad war power that authorizes the President to unilaterally use military force in defense of the United States' national security.[33]

This nuanced construction of the Constitution that arrogated to the American president the unchecked, unbalanced authority to unilaterally use military force in essence extended the shadow of pro-executive precedents like Cincinnatus and *Curtiss-Wright* into the post-9/11 world. To be clear, the omnipotent executive branch is without question one of America's formidable national strengths. It has also historically proven to be one of her exploitable weaknesses when entrusted in unwise hands. As such, the specter of Donald Trump inheriting such power should raise myriad alarms in reasonable minds.

Enemies of the American State: Soviet Union to Al Qaeda to ISIS

Having woven its way through the political philosophies of Machiavelli, Hamilton, and Lincoln, traces of Cincinnatus' legend are discernible in various periods of American national security crisis since World War II.

Consider the Truman administration's declassified 1954 Doolittle report as the Cold War between the United States and Soviet Union heated up. In the way that Cincinnatus led Roman military forces to victory in the battle of Mons Algidus, the Truman administration was preoccupied with charting a course to defeat Soviet communism and the Soviet Union, existential threats perceived to threaten the way of American life. A dictator-like executive branch with the capability to secretly project power globally without the constraints of consent, law, liberal values, and considerations of universal human morality was vital to the CIA's vision of a government that could counter-balance the Soviet Union's desire to globally spread the ideology of communism. As elaborated upon in the Doolittle report:

> [A]nother important requirement is an aggressive covert psychological, political and paramilitary organization more effective, more unique, and if necessary more ruthless than that employed by the enemy ... It is now clear that we are facing an implacable enemy whose avowed objective is world domination by whatever means and at whatever cost. There are no rules in such a game. Hitherto acceptable norms of human conduct do not apply. If the United States is to survive, long-standing American concepts of "fair play" must be reconsidered.[34]

Next, consider a landmark Supreme Court ruling that came down just two decades after the Doolittle report and that commented on our changing form of political organization during times of emergency. Justice Stewart's concurring 1971 opinion in *New York Times Co. v. Sullivan*[35] is exemplary. It ruled that the Nixon administration couldn't block the *Washington Post* and *New York Times* from publishing a leaked copy of the *Pentagon Papers,* a classified national security document analyzing American involvement in secret aspects of anti-communism wars in Southeast Asia. In the opinion, Justice Stewart describes the intensifying quasi-dictatorial character of the Nixon administration's wartime claims to allegedly constitutional

Art. II executive powers. "In the governmental structure created by our Constitution," Justice Stewart wrote,

> the Executive is endowed with enormous power in the two related areas of national defense and international relations. This power, largely unchecked by the Legislative and Judicial branches, has been pressed to the very hilt since the advent of the nuclear missile age.[36]

Here, Justice Stewart stated what was evident then: executive aggrandizement in our constitutional government was a *fait accompli, even* back in the 1970s. More, his description of a Cold War-era executive branch describes a social contract that mirrors those of the dictatorial republics justified in the political thought of Machiavelli, Hamilton and Lincoln.

Having unchecked, unbalanced access to unlimited, unaccountable executive power, naturally, Washington's Cold War-era pattern of secret and selectively illiberal statecraft normalized. It is no surprise that this pattern has persisted in the War on Terror, from 9/11 to the death of bin Laden to the birth of ISIS. The core institutional structure of American government that has been responsible for deciding and executing such policies has not changed since Truman. With the core institutional structure in place – namely, concentrated executive power -- like a step graph, the executive branch has expanded in power and autonomy within the constitutional order during every presidential administration since the end of World War II.

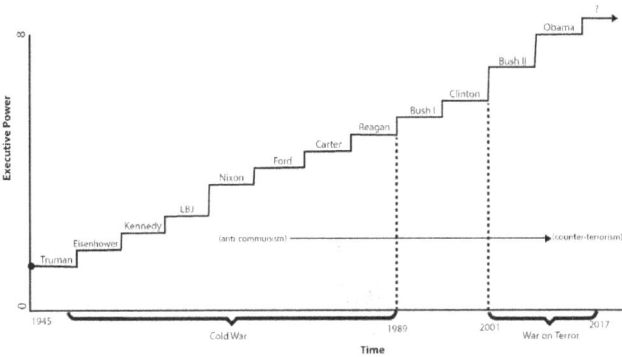

Fig. 6: Step Graph of Executive Usurpations of Power since 1945

Recall, as benevolent dictator, Cincinnatus didn't cling to or seek to extend his ad hoc dictatorship. He gave the dictatorial powers back to the Rome after the crisis ended. To the contrary, and as Figure 6 illustrates, American presidential administrations have done the opposite, each building on the executive usurpations of prior administrations through legislation, executive orders, and unilateralism.

Although America is a liberal democracy in spirit, in between Presidential elections, we, the people, are often kept in the dark. Washington acts secretly, relying on the veritable omnipotence conferred by Art. II executive powers. These tend to be de-linked from consent, shielded from judicial review, and severed from any operational dependency on prior congressional authorization. In other words, Washington can do what it wants, how it wants to, whenever it deems it necessary since during bubbles of crisis, it holds the sword, the purse strings, and the scales of justice that determine the constitutionality of government policy. This contorted scheme of representative government has collapsed the constitutional separation of powers doctrine. It has enabled post-1945 Washington to globally operate more or less like ancient Rome's dictatorial republic during the bubble of crisis.

The proclamations of a long line of post-1945 American presidents reflect the comfort of their unchecked, unbalanced, access to and deployment of the unlimited and expanding power of modern America's executive branch and presidency.

In an infamous 1977 interview with David Frost, President Nixon once exhorted: "[W]hen the president does it, that means it is not illegal."[37] Presidential candidate Trump said something quite similar in the 11th G.O.P debates held in Detroit, Michigan on March 3rd 2016 when pressed by moderator Margaret H. Baier on his support of torture in American national security policies:

> BAIER: Mr. Trump, just yesterday, almost 100 foreign policy experts signed an open letter refusing to support you, saying your embracing expansive use of torture is inexcusable. General Michael Hayden, former CIA director, NSA director, and other experts have said that when you asked the U.S. military to carry out some of your campaign promises, specifically targeting terrorists' families, and also the use of interrogation methods more extreme than waterboarding, the military will refuse because they've been trained to turn down and refuse illegal orders. So what would you do, as commander-in-chief, if the U.S. military refused to carry out those orders?

TRUMP: They won't refuse. They're not going to refuse me. Believe me.

BAIER: But targeting terrorist families?

TRUMP: ... *If I say do it, they're going to do it. That's what leadership is all about.* (emphasis added).[38]

Here, the validity of the corporation-to-nation-state analogy buckles, exposing the inherent limits of the G.O.P presidential candidate's transferrable skill set. To be fair, in his qualified defense, Trump is right, but in another context. The "if-I-say-do-it-they're-going-to-do-it" leadership philosophy is certainly one aspect of what good *managerial* leadership is about in business. The chain of authoritative command in corporate bureaucracies is top-down, just like strong man rule in dictatorships. In the political realm however, that ilk of *presidential* leadership is dictatorial and anti-democratic. This approach to presidential politics is bald anathema to the culture of inter-branch deliberation that constitutionalizes policy in our system of government.

For better or worse, America's executive branch and presidency have become unchecked and unbalanced institutions, acutely so during bubbles of crisis. They possess immense power that can be globally projected in secret policy that can reach Somalia and Afghanistan as easily as Germany or the Spratly Islands in the South China Sea, all carried out without meaningful congressional authorization or judicial review. An executive political culture of implied trust has replaced the normal operation of governmental checks and balances. As a result, American presidential politics in the contemporary age operates on the honor code. Under the honor code, the modern American presidency promises to obey the rule of constitutional law knowing that it probably will never face retributive justice for breaking such promises.

Since the checks and balances in our system of constitutional government have weakened over the Cold War and War on Terror, the American presidency we elect now must vigilantly honor the honor code, like Cincinnatus did in ancient Rome. Will a Trump presidency embrace the legend of Cincinnatus as its political compass? Or is the DNA of Donald Trump more aligned the vices and virtues of Caesar?

4

American Constitutionalism

constitutional crisis \ˌkaːn-stə ˈtuː-ʃən-əl–krī-səs\
(n.) a situation that a legal system's constitution or other
basic principles of operation appear unable to resolve; it
often results in a breakdown in the orderly operation of
government.

The original intent of our Constitution's separation of
powers scheme was to divide our *one* government into
three branches: the executive, the legislature, and the
judiciary. This institutional framework nurtured the real-
time democratic self-regulation of government policy by
positioning each branch to check and balance against the
other within one political system. The three-branch
blueprint was a sagacious reflection by our Founding
Fathers on government design *and* human nature. As
Madison stated in the *Federalist No. 51*:

> Ambition must be made to counteract ambition. The
> interests of the man must be connected with the con-
> stitutional rights of the place. It may be a reflection on
> human nature, that such devices should be necessary
> to control the abuses of government.[39]

Madison's insight was further institutionalized in the 1803
landmark Supreme Court case *Marbury v. Madison*[40] whose
majority opinion that was penned by Chief Justice Marshall
gave birth to the institution of judicial review that has become
as American as apple pie over the years. In Marshall's words,

> It is emphatically the province and duty of the judicial
> department to say what the law is ... A law repugnant
> to the Constitution is void.[41]

Post-*Marbury*, our constitutional government's checks and
balances were set up and have functionally withstood the
test of time and the vicissitudes of American politics.

Our three-branch government as designed in the 18th
century was intended to work as one living organism, like
three chambers of one heart that connects the republic to
the people in real-time. Since 1776 however, this unitary
yet tripartite system of government that was conceived by
the Founders has gradually mutated to comport with an
alternative blueprint that works more like three governance silos in a one vacuum. In this alternative blueprint,
governmental power has disproportionately concentrated
in the executive branch, exacerbating the disconnect
between Washington's policies like torture or dragnet
surveillance and the *vox populi* in the inter-election period.

With such a concentration of power at its disposal, the
executive branch often acts on its own and is accountable
only to itself in particular policy domains. Downstream
risks of executive unilateralism – like the use of the Trump
Card by Donald Trump for instance – are magnified by the
immense executive power that has concentrated in the

American presidency in particular.

On the question of American power in the field of contemporary international relations, America's once peerless dominance as post-Cold War hegemon has declined. Regional competitors in international politics and global markets – from Brazil and Russia to India and China – pose considerable challenges to American global primacy today, circling like ravenous vultures in sight of a meaty carcass. Unlike in the immediate aftermath of the Cold War, the contemporary international system is no longer Washington's oyster.

Be that as it may, America is still a de facto superpower even if she has slowly forfeited her full-spectrum dominance. American strength has reconfigured the de facto political structure of American constitutional government. Essentially, the government design of 18th century America had one blueprint, where the consent of the governed always fueled the government power that formed government policy, as illustrated before in Figure 2. The government design of 21st century America has another, modified blueprint, conceptually illustrated below in Figure 7.

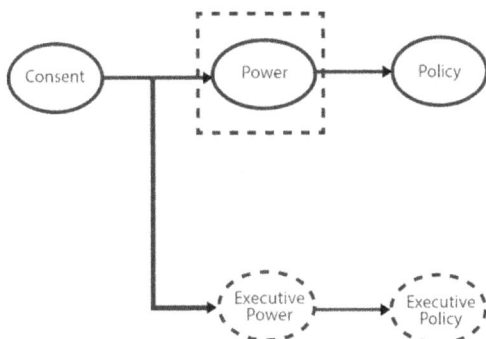

Fig. 7: Consent-to-Policy Flow in Modern
American Government Since 1945

In the 21st century paradigm of American government, executive power is often unchecked and unbalanced within our system of constitutional government. The government we form by ballot no longer faithfully engages in the representative politics of constitutional self-government. Executive power and policy animate a parallel track of governance that has become increasingly impervious to normative constraints like democratic accountability and the rule of constitutional law, which by extension calls into question where our government starts or ends. It is this change in the fundamental way our government is formed and functions that has enabled Washington to increasingly behave like an ad hoc dictatorship during the Cold War and War on Terror. It is this change that has concentrated power in the executive branch at the cost of weakening the structural checks and balances in our 18th century consti-tutional government design that were specifically intended to divide and dilute the executive branch's power and tame its impulses. And ultimately, it is this change in the basic structure of American government that fans the flames of Trumpophobia and feeds the compound fear of a Trump presidency in the public mind.

To be clear, the current evolved form and function of our governmental design in the post-9/11 world has made Washington strong and the people weak during times of emergency. This is not a mistake or failure of our constitu-tional order. Times change. Governments must adapt to keep up. Indeed, our body politic has been changing and adapting since its inception. Converting our social contract to a constitutional democracy under one government was a structural adaptation necessitated by the equation for political survival in the 18th century, illustrated by Benjamin Franklin's well-known phrase, "Join, or Die." popularized after its publication in a political cartoon n the *Pennsylvania Gazette* on May 9, 1754.

J O I N, or D I E.

Fig. 8: "Join, or Die." political cartoon published in the
Pennsylvania Gazette in 1754.

The break away American colonies survived by banding together in a Union. Since 1787, the living mantra of American constitutionalism in our political culture has shifted from "Join, or Die." to "Adapt, or Die."

And the American constitutional order has adapted. Supreme Court Justice Louis Brandeis succinctly articulated this living, breathing – and fundamentally human – aspect of the American constitutional order in an unpublished passage from an early draft of his dissenting opinion in *United States v. Moreland*[42] (1922). "Our Constitution," Brandies writes,

is not a strait-jacket. It is a living organism. As such it is capable of growth – of expansions and of adaptation to new conditions. Growth implies changes, political,

economic, and social. Growth which is significant man-
ifests itself rather in intellectual and moral conceptions
than in material things.[43]

Quite the opposite of a strait jacket, our adaptive Constitution is a living organism, one that has enabled our
government to evolve, to embrace structural elasticity in its
form of political organization, and to permit the weakening
of its checks and balances and the strengthening of its
presidency and executive branch.

The proof of this transformation in our system of constitutional government is in the post-1945 pudding of American
geopolitics. Over the course of the Cold War and War on
Terror, the Constitution has legitimized executive unilateralism, selective illiberalism, government secrecy, and imperial
presidential politics. From the Bay of Pigs to Abu Ghraib,
from drone warfare to dragnet surveillance, the political
sustainability of such American government policies have
been made possible by the changes and adaptations in the
basic structure of our system of constitutional government.
Invariably, these changes and adaptations occur at the nexus
of law and politics in our society.

American legal scholars in the field of constitutional law
theory and American constitutionalism have analyzed this
complex, incendiary relationship. At first glance, at one
end of the spectrum, such an in-depth inquiry into the
American constitutional jurist's mind, the esoteric province
of law professors and Supreme Court justices seems out of
scope for public consumption. Who cares? It is all *way* too
dense to parse and too legalistic to relate to everyday
politics. However, at the other end of the spectrum,

popular conceptions of which government policies are constitutional or unconstitutional are dangerously reductive. If we like a policy, it's constitutional; if we don't like a policy, it's unconstitutional.

Ultimately, there is much more to the constitutionality of a policy than its likability. Constitutional law is inspired by the compass of universal morality but not defined by it. As it turns out, a policy's constitutionality is a moving target on any issue over time. Since 1787, the basic structure of our system of constitutional government has changed through what is called *informal constitutional change.* In the process of informal constitutional change, essentially, the meaning of the Constitution changes through the work of government, outside of courts of law, in the real world, through the administration of policies. It occurs through tangible non-adjudicated acts like Truman sending troops to Korea or Bush committing torture in Guantanamo Bay. The public awareness of informal constitutional change is important for a citizenry to understand the shifting shape of the constitutional government it forms every election.

To be clear, this topic is not novel. Voluminous discussions have already occurred, but they have been confined to the closed circles of America's legal academia, and therefore to this day remain by and large inaccessible to a general readership. As such, before concluding various government policies are constitutional or unconstitutional based on whether we like or dislike them, a brief overview of exemplary scholarship in the area of American constitutional theory is included to introduce the landscape of contemporary American constitutional thought.

These concepts advance our understanding of the Constitution beyond holding a copy of it, and reading the text, written in the 18th century. They will help us understand how the anatomy of our Union that aspires to perfection can change in ways that embolden the republic to project power illiberally during bubbles of crisis, like a dictatorship would. Indeed, Washington has selectively done so since World War II. They also help us understand how Washington has become strong and we, the people, have become weak over the past century. Most importantly, these concepts further deconstruct Trumpophobia.

The American Constitutionalist

Today, the word 'Constitution' is like the word 'love' or 'terrorism', 'beauty' or 'liberty.' It means many things to many people and rarely the same thing to everyone. Prior to the American Revolution, Lord Bolingbroke stated a common understanding of the 18th century definition:

> By constitution, we mean, whenever we speak with propriety and exactness, that assemblage of laws, institutions and customs, derived from certain fixed principles of reason, directed to certain fixed objects of public good, that compose the general system, according to which the community hath agreed to be governed.[44]

In all human societies, public reason and the public good mature as the society modernizes. While they remain fixed within a zeitgeist, they evolve when viewed through a multigenerational prism, from the days of our grandparents' grandparents to our children's children for instance. When the Supreme Court decided *Dredd Scott v. Sanford*[45] *(1857)*, slavery was constitutional and African-Americans were considered movable property rather than humans through the eyes of the law. As the *Dredd Scott* opinion stated, "Negroes" did not migrate to America, they were "imported." Fast forward to 2008. We, the people elected Barack Obama, an African-American, as our first black president.

Things change in unpredictable ways. The collective views on a political issue may harmonize within one generation, but differ across them. The heart of constitutional law theory and American constitutionalism grapple with providing an explanatory framework to capture how this occurs, how the meaning of the Constitution changes over time, and how its changing meaning continues to redefine the relationship between our legal order and our political society.

The works of the following American constitutional law scholars provide a representative microcosm of how American constitutionalism is conceived in American legal academia: David E. Strauss, Jack M. Balkin, Akhil Amar, Bruce Ackerman, Stephen Griffin, and William Eskridge and John Ferejohn. When viewed as a totality, their work provides similar, yet distinct rationales that seek to explain how the Constitution and the American political order have mutually shaped each other since 1787.

Three themes pervade the thinking of these scholars, and form the American constitutionalist view, as it were. First, American politics is governed by the rule of law, and the Constitution is the supreme law of the land. Second, the meaning of the Constitution can change informally through politics and outside of the formal Art. V amendment process that gave us the Bill of Rights which were formal amendments that changed the 1787 Constitution. And third, policies that Washington administers that are not adjudicated *are* presumed to be constitutional. This third factor, what might be called auto-constitutionalization, applies to all of Washington's unadjudicated policies, the good and the bad, the liberal and illiberal.

All three themes shape the American imagination of constitutional government and how it can be used and abused, by a Caesar, a Cincinnatus, a Trump, a Clinton. The ability of the basic structure of system of government to adapt, and endure the various crises of human affairs is the byproduct of informal constitutional change. The ability to change is one of our republic's virtues. It is also one of its exploitable vulnerabilities that Donald Trump has the potential to abuse without obstruction if elected as president of the United States.

One Union, Many Theories

When we think of the Constitution today, three images come to mind. One is of lawyers and their client speaking at a podium on the steps of the Supreme Court, before or after, a politically divisive landmark decision, like a *Roe v. Wade*[46], *Hamdan v. Rumsfeld*[47], *Citizens United v. Federal Election Commission*[48], or *Windsor v. United States*[49]. The second is of a law professor sitting in front of a bookshelf giving a media interview. And the third is typically of an unshaved 2nd Amendment advocate, in a wooded area, giving an interview while holding a hunting rifle and a pamphlet of the Constitution, and talking about the subversive overthrow of the government.

These three images are snapshots of a much bigger constitutional narrative that continues to enrich and organize the norms of American politics. We have one Union under presumably one rule of constitutional law. However, the understanding of how our constitutional order frames our political order in practice, and how the Constitution tames an imperial president or energetic executive bent on illiberal policies is more or less *terra incognita*.

Over the years, American constitutional thought has grappled with tough national questions, from abortion cases like *Roe v. Wade*, enemy combatant cases like *Hamdan v. Rumsfeld*, or same-sex marriage cases like *Windsor v. United States* and *Obergefell v. Hodges*[50].

However, there is a throbbing lacuna. The Supreme Court has not frequently weighed in on national issues of paramount significance such as the contours of presidential war powers or the national security establishment's operational freedoms which include, for example, the targeted killing American citizens on foreign soil by drone strike without due process of law. Generally, Supreme Court jurisprudence is scant on the constitutionality of the executive branch's ability to use military force secretly, illiberally, in violation of international human rights laws, and without requiring congressional approval.

Washington simply does these things and has been with an increasing sense of normalcy since 1945. Today, no universally accepted theory of constitutional law explains the illiberal impulses of our Union's post-1945 national security establishment. Be that as it may, although we have multiple constitutional theories, there is considerable overlap. Each theory in different ways develops an explanation for the constitutional structure of our government and how this structure changes over time in ways that tangibly impact the myriad aspects of our political society.

Let's consider the theory of each scholar in turn. The rationale of each theory concerning informal constitutional change, a real component of our legal order, is foreboding when applied to the prospect of a Trump presidency in 2017. If elected, given the status quo of the American constitutional order, a Trump presidency may be conveniently positioned to opportunistically bend the rule of constitutional law as needs be to rollout national policies like banning Muslims or deporting undocumented immigrants by fiat.

Strauss: Living Constitutionalism

In his book, *Living Constitutionalism*, David Strauss, a law professor at the University of Chicago School of Law, explains living constitutionalism as a theory of constitutional law that posits constitutional meaning changes over time, as our society moves through course of human affairs, from before 1776 to after 9/11. The theory asserts that the Constitution is a 'living' document – a social contract that is a social construct - whose substantive meaning in the legal and political order changes without formal Article V amendments. As Strauss explains,

A 'living constitution' is one that evolves, changes over time, and adapts to new circumstances, without being formally amended. ... The U.S. Constitution is supposed to be a rock-solid foundation, the embodiment of our most fundamental principles: that's the whole idea of having a constitution. Public opinion may blow this way or that, but our basic principles – our constitutional principles – must remain constant.[51]

The unrelenting tension between essential principles of constitutional government and the inherent capriciousness of public opinion animate the yin and yang of American living constitutionalism. It also embodies the potential of American society's social contract to seek equilibrium between the conflicting tensions inherent to political civilization: stasis and flux, anarchic insecurity and principled order, domination and cooperation, the past and the future. Through world wars and economic depression, the nuclear age and terrorist attacks, the Constitution endures. It is the legal nucleus of our political order and rock-solid foundation of principled government.

The meaning of the Constitution matters here, at home, because of its "tremendous presence in our national life." Strauss elaborates:

The living Constitution [is] ... based on an important set of virtues: intellectual humility, a sense of the complexity of the problems faced by our society, a respect for the accumulated wisdom of the past, and a willingness to rethink when necessary and when consistent with those virtues. That is our living Constitution. It makes perfect sense to venerate the Constitution and the people who were responsible for it. But it is important to recognize that the Constitution is the work of more than a few inspired statesmen. It is the work of generations of people – lawyers and nonlawyers, public officials and people living private lives – who have grappled with society's problems and done their best to pass what they learned on to us.[52]

In Strauss's world, the Constitution is not dead. It lives. In Trump's world, the Constitution is simply a non-restraint on executive policy. This view, unfortunately, is not with the general thrust of post-1945 American presidential politics that tends to act first and figure out constitutionality later.

Balkin: Framework Originalism

Jack Balkin presents a similar view on how our Constitution lives as our politics moves from the past to the future. In his theory, framework originalism, Balkin dismisses the ideological irreconcilability of living constitutionalism – which anchors constitutional meaning in the present - and originalism - which anchors it in the 18th century. Instead, in *Living Originalism*, Balkin proposes that both theories of constitutional interpretation are complementary. Like other contemporary American constitutionalists, Balkin develops a framework to analyze the process of constitutional change and meaning that has evolved within the American political order since 1776.

Much of this change is atypical in the legal sense. The change, which is the shadow of the government's exercise of power, generally unfolds outside of the courts and the Article V Amendment process, a phenomenon that has proven to be as much a gift as a curse in hindsight.

In this light, constitutional change in the American political system is dualistic. It occurs inside and outside the Judiciary, everyday. Balkin defines the following three concepts to explain how American government works. As we shall see, while semantics change, the basics concepts do not, and permeate American legal thought on American constitutionalism.

First, Balkin states his view of the Constitution's purpose:

> Constitutions are designed to create political institutions and to set up the basic elements of future political decision-making. Their basic job is not to prevent future decision-making but to enable it. *The job of a constitution, in short, is to make politics possible. This is why constitutions normally protect rights and create structures* ... All three branches of government build institutions and create laws and doctrines that serve constitutional purposes, that perform constitutional functions, or that reconfigure the relationships among the branches of the federal government, the states, and civil society. These activities build out the American state over time. (emphasis added)[53]

Second, Balkin defines constitutional construction, and elucidates its relationship to Strauss' conception of living constitutionalism:

> Living constitutionalism ... is primarily a theory about
> the processes of constitutional development produced
> by the interaction of the courts with the political
> branches. It is a descriptive and normative theory of
> the processes of constitutional construction. It explains
> how change occurs, and it gives an account of why that
> process is democratically legitimate. To understand
> living constitutionalism, therefore, we need to under-
> stand constitutional construction ... Political actors
> engage in constitutional construction when they elabo-
> rate and enforce constitutional values by creating new
> institutions, laws, and governing practices. Constitu-
> tional construction by political actors overlaps with the
> ordinary processes of policy and lawmaking.[54]

The concept of constitutional construction interprets the
Constitution as a blueprint of government design that
helps a people build out their political order based on their
system of law. The legal order sets the boundaries for
building the political order. For example, this idea of
constitutional construction illuminates how our national
security establishment was *constructed*, virtually non-
existent in World War I but veritably omnipresent and
omnipotent today. An outgrowth of Article II executive
power and the National Security Act of 1947 that established the CIA, the Truman administration placed the legal
foundation stones of our embryonic national security
establishment within our political society. The atmosphere
of the Cold War that spanned multiple Presidential
administrations, from Truman to Reagan, provided a
steady supply of geopolitical oxygen at home and abroad

which enabled the national security establishment to expand without check.

As Balking explains, framework originalism,

> views the Constitution as an initial framework for governance that sets politics in motion, and that must be filled out over time through constitutional construction. In implementing the Constitution, later generations must remain faithful to the basic framework, which requires fidelity to original meaning but not the original expected application of the text. This permits a wide range of possible future constitutional constructions that implement the original meaning and that add new institutional structures and political practices not inconsistent with it.[55]

Constitutional construction is a form of democratic state-building. It builds out the nation-state. It socializes the norms and institutions of politics within our framework of governance and law, at home and abroad, from public schools in New Orleans to torture chambers in Guantanamo Bay. Constitutional construction evidences that the anatomy of our Union evolves over time.

Third, in this odyssey of political and constitutional transformation that pervades the American order, evidently, not every issue is adjudicated in our courts. Practically, it can't. The judiciary does not regulate the Republic's projection of power every time it implicates the specific provisions of our Constitution. Doing so would impracticably paralyze government policies with legal tape. As a result, this recurring nexus of projected Article II executive power and its chronic non-adjudication writes what constitutional meaning is by auto-constitutionalizing every act of executive governance by default. This happens even when the government act is illiberal or unconscionable. To accommodate this collateral outcome, the American constitutionalist view generally posits that the Constitution can, and does change, in fundamental ways outside of the judiciary, without formal Article V amendments, affirmatively incorporating liberal, pro-democratic exercises of power while characterizing illiberal exercises of executive power as anomalous, regrettable, or non-existent. Balkin refers to this dialectic as the Constitution-in-practice.

The Constitution-in-practice is:

> a set of laws, institutions, doctrines, and practices that evolve over time ... *[M]ost of the Constitution-in-practice is never interpreted by the courts.* It includes the hardwired parts that nobody ever litigates – for example, the length of the President's term, or the number of houses of Congress. But it also includes other shifting practices that are never litigated. ... Perhaps equally important, there is a law of the executive branch, which includes the construction, over time, of the national security state and the national surveillance state. Although some of the construction is touched on by courts, most of it never is. (italics added)[56]

Overall, Balkin believes that the Constitution is alive like Strauss. It lives with the original principles of our dead Founders. Constitutional meaning shapes the way our legal order sets up our political order. Balkin assumes, as all

American constitutionalists do, that our legal order always organizes our political order, our Constitution is incontrovertibly fundamental, supreme law in American politics, and our field of our legal order is unified, ubiquitous, following the global projection of American power.

Amar: Unwritten Constitution

Akhil Amar, a constitutional law professor at Yale University, advances a concept – the unwritten constitution - in order to explain the generally non-adjudicated patterns of American power within the parameters of the American constitutional order, including those in the domain of foreign affairs and national security. Amar's unwritten constitution *is* Balkin's Constitution-in-practice principle.

Amar defines his concept as follows:

> When viewed properly, America's unwritten constitution supports and supplements the written Constitution without supplanting it ... The written Constitution cannot work as intended without something outside of it – America's unwritten Constitution – to fill in its gaps and to stabilize it. In turn, America's unwritten constitution could never properly ignore the written Constitution, which is itself an integral part of the American experience.[57]

Amar's basic reasoning is the same as Balkin's or Strauss' for that matter. The American constitutional order *must, and always does,* govern the total universe of American governance. To arrive at this view of how the constitutional order shapes politics in Washington, Amar and Balkin assume that in every case, Washington's exercise of non-adjudicated government power is constitutional, whether it is used liberally or illiberally, in conflict or in compliance with American norms, whether it protects human rights in one hemisphere or perpetrates torture in another.

This begs a deeper question: why auto-constitutionalize illiberal power within the American political system in the first place? One motive would seem to have patriotic roots. A secondary motive is likely located in an underlying fear of questioning basic assumptions of our political and constitutional order that have remained more or less untouched since the American Revolution. A constitutional legal theory such as Amar's and Balkin's that auto-constitutionalizes every non-adjudicated act of American government, the good and the bad, is preferable because it is simpler and cohesive.

Any alternative that suggests our government is organized around a system of laws some of the time, and a system of men during bubbles of crisis, would disrupt familiar understandings of American constitutional politics. In such a view, the Constitution is *not* the supreme law of the land and governmental power is not always regulated by the rule of law. This alternative vision of the American constitutional order is detailed further in Chapter 6, and is instructive in understanding the risk that a Trump presidency may pose to the American constitutional order.

Tribe: Invisible Constitution

During the GOP primaries, Trump cited Harvard Law Professor Laurence H. Tribe to attack then presidential candidate Ted Cruz's (R-Tex.) eligibility since Cruz, born in Canada, is not a natural born citizen under any common sense construction of Art. II Sec. 1 Cl. 5.[58] Tribe is an academic expert on American constitutional law. Similar to Balkin and Amar, Tribe also defines a concept of informal constitutional change, what he calls the "Invisible Constitution." While his semantics differ, the overarching theory of the meaning of the Constitution changes dovetails with his American constitutionalist peers. In Tribe's book, *The Invisible Constitution*, the argument he set forth for informal constitutional change seemed by and large intellectually hesitant to articulate a clear, succinct definition of his Invisible Constitution theory. In lieu of one, Tribe describes his search to define the Invisible Constitution as follows:

> I am convinced that the invisible Constitution is at the center of the Constitution's meaning and of its inestimable value ... My hope is to nudge the nation's constitutional conversation away from debates over what the Constitution *says* and whether various constitutional claims are properly rooted in its written text and toward debates over what the Constitution *does*. Put otherwise, I hope to shift the discussion from whether various constitutional claims are properly rooted within the Constitution's written text to whether claims made in its name rightly describe the content, both written and unwritten, of our fundamental law.[59]

What the Constitution *does* in politics often occurs outside of the courts of law, its field of force changing informally in society over time as governance norms do. In this regard, Strauss' living constitutionalism, Balkin's Constitution-in-practice, and Amar's unwritten constitution articulate the same ideas about constitutional change and meaning as Tribe's invisible constitution does.

Eskridge and Ferejohn: small "c" constitutionalism

William Eskridge and John Ferejohn describe American constitutional change in two as having two spaces within which the meaning of the Constitution changed. One occurs formally within the zone of the judicial branch. The call these changes in meaning of the "Large 'C' Constitution.' In contrast, the other space of non-judicial constitutional change is called "small 'c' constitutionalism." Small 'c' constitutionalism is similar to Balkin's Constitution-in-practice and Amar's unwritten constitution.

The authors suggest that their "framework for thinking about American constitutionalism" is "nontraditional," and that a traditional framework typically "emphasizes the words and structure of the Constitution of 1787, especially the Bill of Rights and a few other amendments, as interpreted by judges and trumping the political process." They expand upon their framework as follows:

> Our framework therefore focuses on the primary instruments of the political process itself – statutes, executive orders, congressional-executive agreements, agency rules – and reveals how those political contriv-

ances have become entrenched, indeed to the point of molding the Constitution itself. These devices have evolved from the early days of the republic to permit the protection of an extensive and flexible system of rights and liberties and other forms of security that exist outside the traditional Constitutional frame. Under our account, the primary governmental actors are legislators, executive officials, and administrators, but the ultimate form of political agency is found in We The People, acting through regular elections and the associated devices of political parties but also by means of political associations and interest groups and through popular social movements. The result, which we call small "c" constitutionalism, does not usually operate as a trump card in the way the Large "C" Constitution is thought to act. Instead, it is a modality of public life and discourse, facilitating the building and editing of structures within which we as citizens can live flourishing lives. As a legal matter, small "c" constitutional norms and structures are realities that need to be considered when people and businesses make their plans, administrators implement laws, and judges interpret ordinary statutes and even the Constitution.[60]

Eskridge and Ferejohn distinguish the force of constitutional law within the American political order from the other laws.

A government is constitutional when its ordinary laws and regulations are regulated by higher order norms and not merely by the will of governmental officials. These higher norms may be enforced as laws, as has been true in this country since the founding period, or they may be religious commands characteristic of some natural law theories, or norms of political morality that guide what policy makers do, as has been the tradition in the United Kingdom. But more is expected of a liberal constitution than the mere establishment of a regulatory structure to limit what the majority and its representatives may do. A constitutional democracy also demands that our leaders will be chosen by majorities and will be subject to specific normative guidance as to which norms and rights are constitutionally sacred and what precisely can be done to those in the minority on various issues. In short, democratic constitutionalism requires the following: popular choice of leaders, a normative hierarchy embodying substantive rights, and institutions and procedures for enforcing the hierarchy and at least some of the rights.[61]

Also, similar to Balkin's concept of framework originalism and the role of statutory schemes in constitutional construction that build out a political government while setting principled boundaries on its exercise of power, the authors define the role of statutes in American constitutional and political order.

[S]tatutory rights and structures can go beyond those required by the Constitution ... They interact with Constitutional rights in three ways: 1) statutes transform Constitutional baselines by filling in "huge holes in our governance structure and norms. 2) Legislative and administrative deliberation overtime can create entrenched governance structures and norms—i.e. Civil Rights Act of 1964, Patriot Act 3) The evolution of Large "C" Constitutional law ought to be guided by legislative and administrative deliberation.[62]

Like Balkin and Amar, Eskridge and Ferejohn presume our legal order defines our political order and that our Constitution is fundamental, supreme law that always applies. As discussed earlier, these premises are not always true. More, also like their intellectual peers, their concept of small 'c' constitutionalism sees all acts of executive power as constitutional, including illiberal ones like torture.

Koh: National Security Constitution (NSC)

In synch with the body of Western political philosophy that stretches from Machiavelli and Hamilton to Rossiter, Levinson and Balkin, Yale Law school professor Harold Hongju Koh, a former legal adviser of the State Department under the Obama administration, also generally defends the need for a robust, energetic executive to respond to crisis in the interests of political survival. In his book published in the 1990s, *National Security Constitution,* Koh argues that during crisis, the republic's projection of power can be exercised illiberally and abusively because the executive branch becomes dominant, the Congress becomes acquiescent, and the Judiciary becomes tolerant.

Koh called this effect of crisis on the balance of power within our system of constitutional government, the National Security Constitution (NSC). Koh defines the NSC as follows:

I argue that there lurks within our constitutional system an identifiable National Security Constitution, a
normative vision of the foreign-policy-making process
that emerges only partially from the text of the Constitution itself. Like America's fiscal and administrative
constitution ... the National Security Constitution
comprises that subset of our public law that governs
America's national security decision making ... The
National Security Constitution creates the basic governmental institutions to deal with national security
matters, defines the fundamental power relationships
between those institutions, and places limitations upon
the powers of each branch.[63]

Koh's endorsement of the principle of auto-constitutionalizing
every non-adjudicated act of executive power, even when
exercised in contravention of liberal principles and American
values is a rationale that harmonizes with the American
constitutionalist perspective. The essential logic that enables
American government under the NSC to remain ostensibly
faithful to the constitutional and liberal governance norms is
a concept that Koh calls, *balanced institutional participation.*
Koh elaborates further:

Governmental decisions regarding foreign affairs must
transpire within a sphere of concurrent authority, under
presidential management, but bounded by the checks
provided by congressional consultation and judicial review. In short, the structural principle that animates our
National Security Constitution is balanced institutional
participation ... That legal structure both facilitates and

constrains the operation of the national security policy. This structural vision of a foreign affairs power shared through balanced institutional participation has inspired the NSC since the beginning of the Republic, receiving its most cogent expression in Justice Robert Jackson's famous 1952 Concurring opinion in Youngstown.[64]

Resonating with the works of the aforementioned American constitutionalists, like Balkin, Eskridge, and Frerejohn, Koh's NSC also incorporates the structural variable of 'framework statutes' that modulate constitutional change within the political order. As others postulated, Koh also asserted that in principle and practice, our legal order organizes our political order, always and all the time. Like Balkin's framework originalism, and an example of constitutional construction, framework statutes, Koh writes, "attempt to support the organizational skeleton of the Constitution by developing a more detailed framework for governmental decision-making," and might include: Judiciary Act of 1789, National Security Act 1947, War Powers Resolution 1973, National Emergencies Act 1976, IEEPA 1977.

Koh, also lived through the years of the Nixon and Reagan Presidencies, and experienced the federal government's illiberal exercises of American power abroad during bubbles of Cold War-era crisis in Southeast Asia and Central America. Against this historical context of foreign policy, Koh acknowledges that his concept of balanced institutional participation did not always prevent illiberal projections of power in furtherance of national security objectives. The NSC could enable the republic to mutate into a Cincinnatus-esque benevolent dictatorship, or on the other hand, opt for the path of Caesar. Indeed, during bubbles of post-1945 crises, it is the legacy of Caesar not Cincinnatus that has consistently animated the methods of American geostrategy, even if directed towards the pursuit of liberal objectives and international public goods. Koh explained this recurring pattern in post-1945 American political order sustained such illiberal norms in global policy as follows:

> First ... the president has won because the executive branch has taken the initiative in foreign affairs and has often done so by construing laws designed to constrain his actions as authorizations. Second, the ... for all of its institutional activity, Congress has usually complied with or acquiesced in what the president ahs done, through legislative myopia, inadequate drafting, ineffective legislative tools, or sheer lack of political will. Third, ... because the federal courts have usually tolerated his acts, either by refusing to hear challenges to those acts or by hearing the challenges and then affirming presidential authority on the merits.[65]

Koh's constitutional thinking is still valid today. It captures the essential constitutional dynamics of the War on Terror under the Bush and Obama administrations since 9/11, and into the post-bin Laden age. Koh's conclusion of the permissibility of such executive governance in a liberal political culture presupposes that the American presidency will always be inhabited by Cincinnatus-like leaders. Koh's legitimizing theory of an executive branch that can do what it wants, when it wants, using any means it wants, probably did not reasonably anticipate the election of a presidential candidate such as Donald Trump.

Griffin: Non-Legalized Constitution

Stephen Griffin, a professor at University of Tulane Law School, has been writing about American constitutionalism since the 1990s. I present generous excerpts from his body of work since it captures the essential relationship between the Constitutional and the malleability of the political structure of American government during crisis. Griffin, like Balkin, Koh, and others, has devoted time to attempt to disentangle the tenuous, often contradictory functional relationships between the American constitutional order and the federal government's use of power abroad during crisis. Griffin first defines the prevailing conception of American constitutionalism and the Constitution's role in American politics. "Many scholars," Griffin writes,

> have made two observations about American constitu-
> tionalism: it attempts to use words to create a political
> order, and the artfully designed system of institutions
> specified in the Constitution works to maintain that
> order by dividing and checking political power. The
> latter observation is thus used to explain how the for-
> mer is possible. The problem is that this story does not
> explain how constitutionalism is plausible given the
> pressures exerted by politics and the forces of histori-
> cal change.[66]

In Griffin's view, the Constitution's role in American politics should be parsed through three basic filters: its preordained status as fundamental law, its centrality to the American order, and its subjection to common law judicial review mechanisms since *Marbury v. Madison.* First, concerning the Constitution's preordained status, Griffin asserts that,

> [t]he basic idea of American constitutionalism is conducting government under the provisions of a fundamental law ... Article VI of the United States Constitution proclaims it to be the "supreme law of the land." This signals the primary characteristics of American constitutionalism. It is based on a written document that is the fundamental law of the republic. These two characteristics are reinforcing.[67]

Noteworthy, the presumed supremacy and fundamentality of constitutional law in the American order is a sine qua non of the American constitutionalist's view. Griffin's definition mirrors this prevailing consensus, echoing the general accepted views of the Constitution in our political order.

Another point Griffin raises is the intrinsic structural non-enforceability of the Constitution and the constitutional order in circumstances when the government chooses not to respect its provisions. This occurs when Washington acts alone and is accountable to itself, a political scenario that pierces to the heart of Trumpophobia. The Constitution, despite its presumptive supremacy, has demonstrably proven vulnerable to systematic non-enforcement by

Washington. At best, the Take Care clause of Art. II that requires the president to faithfully execute the laws has been selective observed. This selective and systematic non-enforceability of constitutional law liberates the republic's exercise of power from the system of law intended to constrain it. This behavior is reinforced by the absence of an 'external agency' to make sure the political system as a whole conforms to the Constitution. Griffin elaborates,

> When an individual violates a law, the government stands ready to enforce the law and remedy the violation. There is no parallel to this situation in the constitutional sphere. There is no agency external to the federal government that stands ready to enforce the Constitution when a branch of that government violates the Constitution. We may immediately think of judicial enforcement of the Constitution, but this response misses the point. Just as it is possible for any individual to violate the law, it is possible for any branch of government (including the judiciary) to violate the Constitution. The difference is that although the government stands ready to enforce the law against any individual, there is no government agency with a similar power to enforce the Constitution. The checks and balances the Constitution provides are no remedy when all branches are in violation of the Constitution.[68]

Generally in conformity with his peers, Griffin also articulates a conception of informal constitutional change. Legal scholars differ in semantics, but generally agree that constitutional meaning changes outside the Article V amendment process, non-judicially and outside the Court, but still within the fundamental boundaries of the constitutional order and system of government. This is a view that echoes the essence of Balkin's Constitution-in-practice, Amar's unwritten constitution, and Eskridge and Frerejohn's small 'c' constitutionalism. Griffin calls this category of constitutional change, the 'non-legalized constitution.'

> A constitution is legalized to the extent that it is made cognizable by lawyers and courts ... Within the sphere of the legalized Constitution, decisions by the judiciary are regarded as authoritative ... Constitutional change can occur through either a legal (formal) or non-legal (informal) process. Legal change, change within the legalized Constitution, can occur through amendment or judicial interpretation. Non-legal constitutional change occurs through the political process.[69]

Thematic Troika

On balance, from Balkin to Griffin, the American constitutionalist view agrees on three common points. The Constitution is the supreme law of the land; the meaning of the Constitution can informally change through politics and outside of the formal Art. V amendment process; every unadjudicated governmental policy is presumptively constitutional, even if it patently violates American values and internationally-recognized human rights, like torture or extra-judicial killings, drone warfare or dragnet surveillance.

These governance norms are now woven in the fabric of the American constitutional order. They are fair game for a Trump administration.

While neglected or avoided in mainstream political commentary, the soul of Trumpophobia emanates from the basic fact that the government that a Trump administration would take control of is significantly different in size, concentrated executive power, and institutional design than the one conceived of in 1787. The one we have now operates under norms of executive unilateralism and security sculpted by the Cold War and War on Terror. It has a strong presidency and weak checks and balances.

To this extent, while Trump's campaign pledges to bomb brown families on foreign soil or ban Muslims seem extreme and outrageous, on their face, they are not constitutionally impermissible. Indeed, Donald Trump might argue such policies are relatively tame when compared to Nixon's carpet bombing of Cambodia, Reagan's funding of paramilitaries in Guatemala and Nicaragua, or Bush's use of waterboarding in Cuba. If he were to, although disagreeable and morally objectionable, he would make a fair point. Maybe banning Muslims from American soil is less unconscionable than torturing them in counter-terrorism interrogations.

This is a slippery Hobbesian slope with Faustian bargains all the way down. Trump may be willing to make them all as president of the United States.

5

The Anti-Supremacy Thesis

law \\lo\\
(n.) 1. That which is laid down, ordained, or established;
2. A system of principles and rules of human conduct,
being the aggregate of those commandments and principle which are either prescribed or recognized by the
governing power in an organized jural society as its will
in relation to the conduct of the members of such society, and which it undertakes to maintain and sanction
and to use as the criteria of the actions of such members.

If the boundaries of the Constitution were enforceable,
and if the checks and balances of our system of government could be relied upon to tame and civilize a Trump
presidency, Trumpophobia might be less of a concern in
this election. Normally, presidential elections provide a
televised public ring for the embattled Democrat-
Republican fight for the Oval Office. Normally, in this
mono y mono human fight for the Oval Office, the fate of
the Constitution does not hang in the balance as it does
now in this presidential election.

So, what happens when the rule of constitutional law
ceases to regulate pockets of American life and selected
domains of government policy?

Anti-supremacy politics.

Anti-supremacy politics delineates a circumscribed space in a law-bound political society in which anarchy has supplanted order in certain policy areas. Here, government power is unlimited and governmental institutions are unchecked. Such a space exists in modern America, for instance, in the policy areas of foreign affairs and national security that affects innocent civilians abroad, or policy areas like racialized police brutality that affects civilians at home. Here, a Trump presidency would present considerable risks to disrupt and destabilize settled norms of the American constitutional order.

If you are still not even mildly petrified or concerned now, well, keep reading.

The Perils of Anti-Supremacy Politics

Our notion that checks and balances *still* check and balance the executive branch in the American system of government was a reasonable assumption back in the 18th century. Today, it is not. To sustain this belief in the age of contemporary American politics requires a quantum leap of constitutional faith. The assumption that governmental policy is checked and balanced by other branches does not persuasively explain the way that Washington actually works in practice, particularly in the policy domains of foreign affairs and national security.

This belief that government policy is checked and balanced within our constitutional order is perpetuated by our liberal political tradition that *believes* in the rule of law. It is also sustained by the ubiquitous view that our Constitution is the supreme law of the land today, just as it was in 1787, as textually set forth in the Supremacy Clause of Art. VI of the Constitution.

This deferential belief in the rule of law is misleading. A side effect, the dubious sacrosanctity of constitutional supremacy it breeds dangerously assuages the perceived risks that a Trump presidency poses to our constitutional order. It's similar to believing that the RMS Titanic was not sinking *after* it hit that iceberg on the cold night of April 14, 1912. When the RMS Titanic hit an iceberg and if you were a passenger, it would have been better to know of the collision than to have remained in the dark, enjoying the string quartet instead of preparing for the ship to sink in frigid waters. In any scenario, knowledge of danger is better than clinging to the illusion of safety in times of peril. Similarly, if our constitutional government's checks and balances as designed in 1787 have become substantially weaker in the post-9/11 world, and our constitutional order is sinking in tangible ways that endanger us here and now, it is better to know than to close our eyes, pretend everything is okay, and relax in the dark while we enjoy the string quartet.

Our rule of constitutional law is not a *fact.* It is a *commitment.* It is not an immutable, feature of our system of government. It is an aspiration. Our political culture's infidelity to the law's spirit seduces its decay, and ultimately its death as a social force capable of shaping the politics of government. When the rule of constitutional law dies in whole or substantial part, anti-supremacy politics rises like a Phoenix from its ashes.

The Anti-Supremacy Thesis aims to simplify our prevailing understanding of constitutional politics by advancing a simple proposition that pierces through the fog of law in political life: the Constitution of the United States is *not* the supreme law of the land all the time, especially when it is left systematically unenforced by the government in the event of breach from conduct by citizens or the incumbent administration itself. The Constitution may have been supreme law once. It no longer vigilantly is in all policy domains today.

This is because the government no longer faithfully enforces the Constitution with sufficient vigilance to render it supreme or with sufficient regularity to render it a binding rule. In fact, the government not infrequently moonlights as the lawbreaker itself. In truth, the Constitution does not always follow the flag at home or abroad in the contemporary age. In the practice of American politics, sometimes it does. Other times it doesn't. Such enforcement irregularities in American politics have effectively nurtured pockets of anarchy in spaces where constitutional law does not regulate government policy. Moments in governance when the law does not regulate politics open up spaces for abuse of government power by an imperial presidency or secretive and energetic executive branch.

This is anti-supremacy politics in a nutshell.

It has thrived in the American constitutional order at least since 1945, from Truman to Obama. In anti-supremacy politics, if the Constitution is not vigilantly enforced, not only is it not supreme law – it is not law at all as a matter of jurisprudence. Here, the Constitution devolves into text without power in political space, like any other ordinary unenforced law would. The proximate cause of this degeneration results from a chronic presidential legal culture of persistent non-enforcement of certain laws, that choose to honor Art. II's Take Care Clause in the breach.

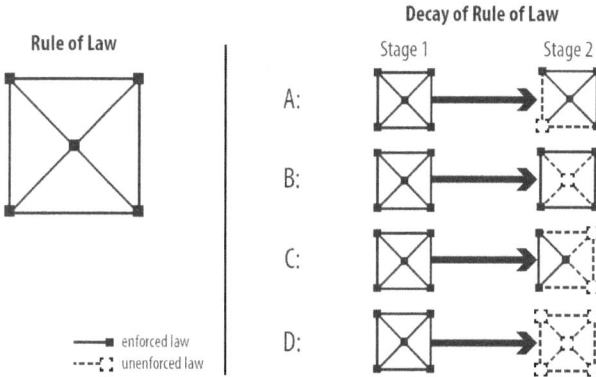

Fig. 9: Anti-Supremacy Thesis

Shown in Figure 9, anti-supremacy politics nurtures the partial or full collapse of the rule of law in all governments, including constitutional liberal democracies like America's. Unenforced laws are interdependent and become non-existent in politics, replacing order with anarchy in the policy areas once governed by them. Absent a political culture that vigilantly enforces its rule of law, the government, once a system of laws, becomes, a system of men in the policy domains in which the law has collapsed due to selective non-enforcement. The rule of law ends up ruling over certain policies and not others, certain neighborhoods and not others. This culture of selective non-enforcement creates anarchic pockets of governance within the political order that often dovetail with policy domains like national security or foreign affairs.

This tangible effect of anti-supremacy politics in American

life enables an otherwise democratic government to slouch into the governance routines of ad hoc dictatorship because the Constitution no longer vigilantly polices and nourishes the structure of government or form and function of political organization. Said otherwise, policy areas where Washington can do what it wants, when it wants, and however it wants, unconstrained by the consent of the governed or liberal values are typically policy areas where the rule of law – including the Constitution – has collapsed, at least in substantial part. Here, anti-supremacy politics fills the vacuum.

While absent from contemporary interpretations of American constitutional politics, the Anti-Supremacy Thesis is not a novel notion. Rather, it is more of a forgotten one. Recall Hamilton in *Federalist No. 15* who once observed,

> [g]overnment implies the power of making laws. It is essential to the idea of a law, that it be attended with a sanction; or, in other words, a penalty or punishment for disobedience. If there be no penalty annexed to disobedience, the resolutions or commands which pretend to be laws will, in fact, amount to nothing more than advice or recommendations.[70]

Nineteenth century British jurist John Austin, a founder of the school of legal positivism, defined law as the command of the sovereign, backed up by sanctions. Many legal philosophers before and after Hamilton and Austin have echoed the same common sense views. A law – even if the Constitution – that is chronically left unenforced by the government is no law at all, and *not* part of the rule of law that organizes the system of government. This attribute is exacerbated when the government – the law enforcer – moonlights as the lawbreaker. No actor in the institutional design of the government can stop the government from violating its own laws.

Foreign targets of American national security policies often feel the wrath of anti-supremacy politics, from Yemeni civilian victims of misguided American drone strikes in remote villages, to Arab-Muslim individuals tortured in black sites like Guantanamo Bay in Cuba or Bagram Air Base in Afghanistan. At home, the Black Lives Matter movement is exemplary of a social movement response to the sense of citizen powerlessness felt here at home as a result of the anti-supremacy politics of government security forces . The prevalent example is the lawlessness of the culture of white police brutality that targets black communities, often resulting in the unpunished murder of young, male black citizens, from Michael Brown in Ferguson, Missouri to Eric Garner in Staten Island, New York, Sylville Smith in Sherman Park, Milwaukee to Freddie Gray in Baltimore, Maryland, to Philando Castile in St. Anthony, Minnesota. In this regard, the deaths of a Yemeni civilian or Philando Castile are byproducts of the same anti-supremacy politics: the government's violent use of force that is not constrained by the Constitution and is not punished after the fact.

We see the same brand of anti-supremacy politics in post-1945 American foreign affairs and national security. Consider the following breakdown of the post-9/11 Bush administration's compliance with the rule of constitutional law in a process of decay.

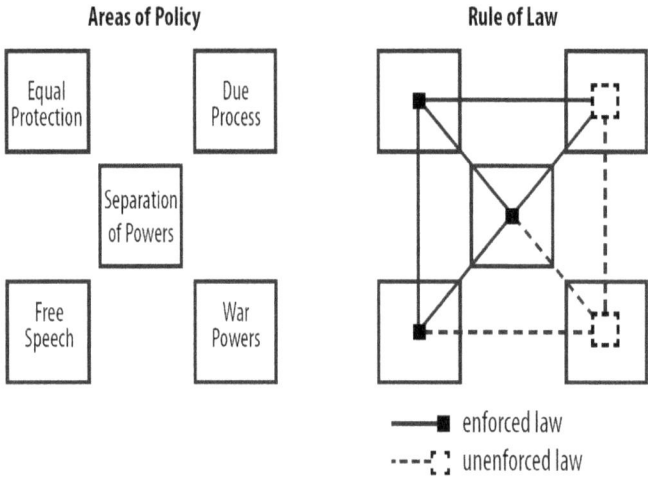

*Fig. 10: Anti-Supremacy Thesis and Post-9/11
American Counterterrorism*

As illustrated in Figure 10, the rule of constitutional law slowly breaks down and decays in areas like war powers, and due process, the government slowly becomes un-checked and unbalanced. As it does, anti-supremacy politics begins to thrive.

The perils of anti-supremacy politics further legitimize the fears embodied in the epidemic of Trumpophobia. Extrapo-lating from his campaign pledges, a Trump presidency cannot be reasonably expected to observe or faithfully preserve the American constitutional order. The potentially global ramifications of this specter are frightening in light of the GOP presidential nominee's unpredictability and the American presidency's omnipotence.

Rule of Auto-Constitutionality

Sometimes, a government does not enforce the Constitution, creating pockets of anarchy in our political society and converting our government back to a system of men vis-à-vis certain policy domains. This is the Anti-Supremacy Thesis in a nutshell. Other times, every act of government that is unadjudicated is deemed constitutional, even if it is unlawful or illiberal on its face, like torture. In a nutshell, this is the result of a phenomenon I call auto-constitutionality which poses dangerous risks to our norms of American politics if an anti-Cincinnatus figure like Donald Trump wins the presidential election.

Auto-constitutionality is a legal principle that permeates ordinary politics. It is a norm in our political culture that deems acts of government constitutional because they occurred and were never determined to be unconstitutional through adjudication. In other words, they are presumptively constitutional because a court of law never ruled them unconstitutional. This happens all the time.

The non-exhaustive list of concepts, including Balkin's Constitution-in-Practice, Amar's unwritten constitution, Eskridge and Ferejohn's small 'c' constitutionalism, Griffin's non-legalized constitution, and other variations such as Tribe's invisible constitution, are all essentially interchangeable in one aspect.

They all auto-constitutionalize the federal republic's exercise of Article II executive power. Nixon's bombing of Cambodia, Reagan's funding of paramilitaries in Central America, Bush's use of torture, and Obama's use of drone warfare and warrantless global electronic surveillance are all examples of Balkin's Constitution-in-practice, Amar's unwritten constitution, Koh's NSC, Schlesinger's Imperial Presidency, Eskridge and Ferejohn's small "c" constitutionalism, Griffin's non-legalized constitution, and Tribe's invisible constitution.

Each American scholar implicitly advances the theoretical premise – a dangerous one – of auto-constitutionality. As the meaning of the Constitution within the American order changes over time and outside the courts and Article V Amendment process, and as every act of government cannot be adjudicated for its constitutionality, our legal order assumes that acts of government that are never adjudicated *are* constitutional.

To be clear, pragmatic politics compels us to auto-constitutionalize unadjudicated acts of government policy, whether it is sending humanitarian aid to Africa or torturing alleged non-white enemy combatants in Cuba. Indeed, determining the constitutionality of every act through judicial review would be impractical and untenable, choking the engine of government with legal tape. We just have to assume the government we elect will be faithful to the Constitution while it is in power. However, this turns problematic when illiberal, unconscionable governmental acts, like torture or like dragnet surveillance are auto-constitutionalized due to absence of adjudication.

The risk, however, is that this governance norm essentially empowers the executive branch to write law. The auto-constitutionalization of Article II executive power in the domain of national security and foreign affairs routinely effectuates constitutional change and sets constitutional meaning, even when such power fuels unconscionable policies that violate basic American values.

The premise of auto-constitutionality nurtures a zone within our system of government in which the executive branch bypasses the judiciary and legislature and decides constitutional meaning with precedential value for itself, outside of the courts, outside of Article V Amendment process, and outside of the inter-branch deliberation between the executive branch and legislature that is supposed to anchor constitutional politics.

The executive branch has auto-constitutionalized American selective illiberalism over a century of statecraft now. American legal and constitutional thinking – embodied in the American constitutionalist view - largely deal with this issue by turning a blind eye, or what in academia is referred to as the canon of constitutional avoidance. In this view, the regrettable outlier of American selective illiberalism is deemed constitutional because it is never ruled to be unconstitutional through judicial review. This approach to American constitutionalism advances the following axiom: non-judicial constitutional change is *never* unconstitutional, including when it is singularly authored by the policy hand of the executive branch. The analytical reflex compels us to "fill in the gaps," in the American constitutional order, as Amar articulated, and create concepts like the "Constitution-in-practice," "unwritten constitution," "invisible constitution", "small 'c' constitutionalism", and the "non-legalized Constitution."

On the one hand, these concepts are necessary to enable American legal theory to explain how constitutional norms have changed over time without formal Art. V amendment.

Theoretically, they integrate the face of America at her best in the constitutional order. However, informal constitutional change also includes America at her worst. Under these same concepts like the Balkin's "Constitution-in-practice", Amar's "unwritten constitution", or Tribe's "invisible constitution," the Bay of Pigs and Abu Ghraib *were* constitutional. American torture, including the waterboarding of Khaled Sheik Mohammed or CIA's blunt instrument sodomy of El-Masri *is* constitutional. The targeted killing of American citizens on foreign soil by drone strike and without due process of law *is* constitutional. Dragnet surveillance and force-feeding hunger strikers *is* constitutional.

And so on.

The basic components of a political order – like the law, the rule of law, the Nation – are born and die in the minds of the people, a sentiment succinctly put by judge Learned Hand:

> [l]iberty lies in the hearts and minds of men and women; when it dies there, no constitution, no law, no court can save it.[71]

The same holds true for the Constitution. It lives and dies in the hearts and minds of the citizenry. However, a constitutional order does not possess a binary fate that oscillates between life and death. It can grow or decay as our Union and we, the people, have. Compartmentalized atrophy within the legal order is not only possible, it is the constitutional norm. Systems of law, like any social construct that generates desirable collective norms of citizen behavior in political society, generally do not die in a singular *coup de grace.* Rather, they may decay slowly in different zones of subject matter over time, as the norm of non-enforcement replaces the norm of a binding rule of law whose breach is vigilantly remedied by the government.

Today, our rule of constitutional law is concurrently supreme and non-supreme in different fields of policy. It is consistently enforced in certain areas of policy like freedom of speech and consistently unenforced in other policy areas like national security. The mosaic of policy areas where our rule of constitutional law is non-supreme is where anti-supremacy politics reign, and where Washington can do what it wants, when it wants, using any means it wants, as a dictatorship would.

It is in such political spaces where the prospect of a Trump presidency feels frightful and the prospect of constitutional crisis imminent if Trump were to be elected as president.

A government that embraces anti-supremacy politics knowingly nurtures issue-based anarchy in its domestic political order, even if said government gives lip service to the rule of law in public messaging. The norms of anti-supremacy politics tend to extricate government policy from rules and principles of self-restraint that would otherwise regulate the exercise of power or formulation of policy, be it morality or constitutional law, democratic consent or liberal values. For instance, consider the anti-supremacy politics of a Donald Trump, who has pledged to build a U.S-Mexico wall, ban Muslims, and deport millions of illegal immigrants. The American constitutional order will struggle to tame and civilize him vis-a-vis these campaign pledges that may morph into government policies in 2017. Sure, we can vote Donald Trump in to the Oval Office, but anti-supremacy politics will just as surely make it arduous for our Constitution to tame and civilize Trump once he inherits the unaccountable power that comes with the American presidency.

6

Constitutional Dictatorship

elasticity *i-las-ti-sə-tē*\
(n.) 1. the ability of an object or material to resume its
normal shape being compressed or stretched; 2. the ability of something to change and adapt

---

Although America is a liberal democracy, we are
familiar with politics of dictatorial rule during times of
emergency. The American people have re-experienced
Washington's unilateral use of Article II executive power
during every bubble of crisis since World War II. Of
course, this reflex of our republic is not surprising.

From the historical perspective of government design,
republics, empires, and dictatorships have always had one
thing in common – their social contracts define a form of
political organization that is based on centralized and
concentrated power. In each of these political systems,
political power aggregates in one place, like a republic or a
strong man. In that place, one entity has the authority to
use that power. When that same political entity that is
authorized to use such power is also the designated authority to enforce the rule of law that regulates the use of that
power, what we have is a structural conflict of interest.

What results is an unchecked, unbalanced form of political organization. Here, we can see that the bright-line boundary between constitutional democracy and elective dictatorship invariably begins to get fuzzy as the executive branch's power increases in concentration and the enforcement of the rule of law decreases in regularity.

Under such conditions, constitutional democracies can fluidly morph into constitutional dictatorships. As generally understood, a government's routine martyring of liberty on the altar of security is the insignia of authoritarian governance in military dictatorships, not liberal democracies. This tenuous balance between civil liberty and national security has invited impassioned discussion in post-9/11 America in light of policies under the Bush and Obama administrations such as torture and dragnet surveillance. The incumbent administration defends its executive unilateralism by arguing balancing security and liberty is a zero-sum game. The need for more of one necessitates compromising the other, the government argues. This framework is misguided because it omits the most salient fact: in American government, the security-liberty balancing that occurs in the formulation of government policy must unfold within the confines of the constitutional order.

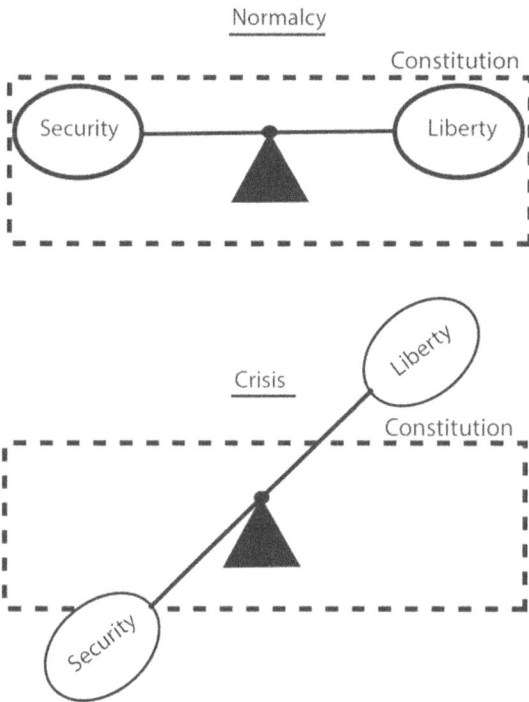

Fig. 11: The Security-Liberty Balance in American Constitutional Politics.

Figure 11 illustrates the zero-sum equation of security-liberty balancing within a constitutional system of government, wherein more liberty is less security, and vice versa. Even if Washington does sacrifice liberty for security, this trade-off must occur within the boundaries of the constitutional order. The Constitution places inviolable limits on the extent to which Washington can sacrifice liberty in the name of security. However, when anti-supremacy politics reigns, and the American constitutional order no longer regulates security-liberty balancing in the formulation of government policy, Washington makes unconstitutional trade-offs between these competing interests, and America's slide from constitutional democracy to constitutional dictatorship becomes more and more slippery. Such has been the case in post-1945 America, and will likely recur in the event that Donald Trump is elected as president of the United States.

Interestingly, the analogy between liberal democracy and benevolent dictatorship as an explanatory model for American power in foreign affairs and national security has been obstinately dismissed in the West --- like alleging the world is round when everyone believes it to be flat.

Since America is considered a democracy, the constitutional dictatorship thesis, even when reasonably applicable in the post-1945 American context, remains intellectually objectionable. Outside the context of conspiracy theory, the notion has never entered American mainstream political debate. The rationales that compare a constitutional democracy and constitutional dictatorship are rejected on varying grounds. They don't neatly fit into liberal theories of politics or constitutional law. They are ostracized as biased and prejudicial leftist rants unworthy of merit. They are pegged as ideologically bankrupt on the flawed, semi-patriotic premise that any government that was once born a democracy and that continues to hold elections can never devolve into a dictatorship.

The dismissal of the constitutional dictatorship thesis is additionally flawed because it supposes America is a pure democracy. It is not now. It never was. True, America *was* born and still *is* a democracy, but the federal government in Washington is a republic, a part of the democracy-republic chimera that emanates from the American constitutional order. In this regard, from a structural perspective, the social contact of a republic can morph into dictatorial embodiments to meet the exigencies of crisis, especially in between election cycles. They can because republics and dictatorships are based on similar conceptions of centralized power, be it a strong man or a governmental entity. Exemplified by the legend of Cincinnatus in ancient Rome, a democratic republic can wax dictatorial during crisis. If we consider the modern American example, arguably every elected American presidential administration during the Cold War and War on Terror has demonstrated the same elasticity that permits Washington to wax dictatorial in between elections. And when Washington does, the surge of energy that flushes the veins of the executive branch to address threats posed by a crisis can ephemerally turn America's constitutional democracy into a constitutional dictatorship, just the way the Cincinnatus transformed the Roman Republic.

Ducks and Gorillas

Thought Experiment: If you *see* a duck and *call* it a gorilla, does that make the duck a gorilla?

Hopefully, your answer is no. Labels like duck or gorilla are just words. They purport to describe what things are. Labels – correct or incorrect – cannot ever actually *change* in fact what a thing *is*. So, if the animal you see looks like a duck, walks like a duck, and talks like a duck, most likely it is not a gorilla. The rational inference is that most likely, the animal you are observing is a duck. Indeed, it is still a duck even when your neighbor prefers to repeatedly call it a gorilla. The animal is a duck because it has duck DNA.

Labeling the type of government we live under presents a similar tension in how public debate and political vocabulary label the form of political organization that is based on the evolving blueprint of our living social contract. For instance, during times of emergency, if we experience the politics of a dictatorship and call it democratic, does that make dictatorial rule democratic? No. It shouldn't. Dictatorial rule is dictatorial in fact, even if your neighbor repeatedly calls it democratic. The DNA of a government is its living social contract that defines how the powers of government and liberties of citizens relate within the evolving blueprint of one political society. If a government looks, feels, and functions like a dictatorship, and that government exhibits dictatorship DNA, then that government is a dictatorship even if everyone you know calls it a democracy.

During the Cold War and War on Terror, American liberal democracy has often looked, felt, and functioned like a constitutional dictatorship during bubbles of crisis when the executive branch is active and energetic and its policies are increasingly characterized by secrecy and unilateralism. To be clear, does this mean that Washington has ruled like a dictatorship in all aspects of government policy? No, it hasn't. But has Washington selectively exhibited dictatorial impulses in foreign affairs and national security over the course of the Cold War and War on Terror, from the Bay of Pigs to Abu Ghraib to drone warfare and dragnet surveillance? Yes, it has.

The label of pure democracy no longer accurately describes contemporary Washington's chronic propensity for non-representative, secret, and selectively illiberal policies during crisis, the formulation and execution of which are neither constrained by consent, law, or liberal values. As a result, our constitutional democracy often moonlights as an ad hoc constitutional dictatorship during times of emergency.

Our government makes this democracy-to-dictatorship transformation even if we always label our politics as democratic and never as dictatorial. Indeed, three American political and legal philosophers – Clinton Rossiter, and more recently Yale University law professor Jack M. Balkin and University of Texas law professor Sanford V. Levinson – have made this connection of dictatorial rule in democratic politics. In concert, Rossiter, Balkin, and Levinson all defend the politics of constitutional dictatorship in a democratic society.Their arguments are set forth below. That said, they also probably never anticipated the viability of a black swan presidential candidate such as Donald Trump *ever* actually contending for the Oval Office.

Of Dictatorship and Democracy

In his book, *Constitutional Dictatorship*, published in 1948, Rossiter described how a democracy can turn dictatorial under particular circumstances. As Rossiter observed in the post-World War II climate of fear and superpower competition, in countries like England, France, Germany, and the United States, the rules that governed political decisional autonomy within a constitutional government could and should consolidate in one place during crisis.

This reconfiguration of power within the constitutional order made the republic strong and the people weak in ways that benefitted the society as a whole. According to Rossiter, the dictatorship option is the *sine qua non* of a democracy's political survival, a view that echoes Lincoln after the American Civil War. Rossiter suggested that "no form of government can survive that excludes dictatorship when the life of the Nation is at stake" but at the same time, Rossiter conceded the manifest unpopularity of dictatorial politics in a democratic society:

> [n]o person professing the democratic faith can take much delight in a study of constitutional dictatorship; the fact remains that it has been with us exactly as long as constitution government, and has been used to all times, in all free countries, and by all free men.[72]

Rossiter defines Constitutional Dictatorship in the following passage:

> The dictator in Mr. Webster's dictionary is primarily 'one appointed to exercise, or one exercising, absolute authority in government, especially in a republic.' Indeed, the qualifying adjective constitutional is almost redundant, for the historical conception of dictatorship was that it could not be other than constitutional. The original dictatorship, that of the Roman Republic, involved the legal bestowal of autocratic power on a trusted man who was to govern the state in some grave emergency, restore normal times and government, and hand back this power to the regular authorities just as

soon as its purposes had been fulfilled. *The phrase constitutional dictatorship, hyperbole though it may be in many
instances, will serve as the general descriptive term for the
whole gamut of emergency powers and procedures in periodi-
cal use in all constitutional countries, not excluding the
United States of America.* (emphasis added)[73]

As Rossiter elaborates, after a political society's democratic
transition to a constitutional dictatorship in response to crisis,

[t]he government meets the crisis by assuming more
powers and respecting fewer rights ... The result is a re-
gime which can act arbitrarily and even dictatorially in
the swift adoption of measures designed to save the state
and its people from the destructive effects of the particular crisis. And the narrow duty to be pursued by this
strong government, this constitutional dictatorship?
Simply this and nothing more: *to end the crisis and restore
normal times* ... In short, the aim of constitutional dictatorship is the complete restoration of the *status quo ante
bellum.*[74]

The constitutional dictatorship's roots in ancient Rome
and the legacy of Cincinnatus support its ostensible
desirability as a model of political government. However,
American presidents from Truman to Obama have used
the pretext of crisis to expand executive power, a pattern
that would be likely to continue under a Trump presidency.
Rossiter also outlines the regulations and procedures
that governed the Roman Republic's transition to ad hoc
Roman Dictatorship:

[t]here did exist in ancient Rome a political phenomenon, the dictatorship, whereby in time of crisis an
eminent citizen was called upon by the ordinary officials of a constitutional republic, and was temporarily
granted absolute power over its whole life, not to sub-
vert but to defend the republic, its constitution, and its
independence.[75]

To be sure, once the Roman dictatorship was in force, and
the "Imperium" had been "conferred" to the dictator, "the
dictator became as absolute a ruler as could well be imag-
ined."[76] For example, while "[a]ccording to Roman
constitutional law the dictator could not legislate, that is,
initiate and promulgate a lex," the dictator did possess "the
ius edicendi, and his decrees were, for the duration of his
power, as good as laws and were published as such. *Quod
dictatori placuit legis habet vigorem.*"[77]

The dictatorship that emerged from the republic during
crisis was also subject to principled limitations set forth in
controlling law. These enforceable limitations helped to
counterbalance the concentration of power in one ruling
entity, and had three aspects. First, two consuls of the
Senate jointly made the ultimate decision to invoke the
Republic's dictatorial powers:

[w]henever the Senate was convinced that the Republic
was in grave danger and that the ordinary hierarchy of
administrative officials was not competent to secure its
safety, it could initiate a proposal that the consuls appoint a dictator. The consuls themselves could also
propose that the dictatorship be employed, but the

approval of the Senate remained necessary. The power of appointment resided constitutionally in the two consuls. They might act jointly, often in consultation with the praetor, or separately, in which case the consul who made the appointment was chosen by lot. In the selection of the dictator the consul followed the consul followed peculiar religious rites to which he alone was competent. This prevented an unconstitutional appointment of a dictator ... The citizen selected as dictator had his Imperium, his sacred and absolute power, conferred upon him by a *lex curiata*, a matter of form only, but a constitutional procedure that gave the particular dictatorship its stamp of legality. The whole process of instituting the dictatorship rarely consumed more than two or three days.[78]

Second, the dictatorship was governed by law: the *lex curiata* defined its purpose; the *dictature rei ferundae causa* applied to matters of Roman security abroad; the *dictature seditionis sedandae* applied to Roman security at home.

The *lex curiata* which gave legal sanction to the particular dictatorship defined the purpose of its institution. There were two varieties of constitutional dictatorship for time of crisis in Rome, the *dictature rei gerundae causa* (literally, "the dictatorship for getting things done") and the *dictatura seditionis sedandae et rei gerundae causa* ("the dictatorship for suppressing civil insurrection"). Out of the total of about ninety dictatorships recorded in the three hundred year history of the office, approximately fifty were *rei gerundae causa*. This was the appellation affixed to the true Roman dictator, the man called upon by the people to assume all powers and save the state from the threat of total defeat in war.[79]

Third, the dictatorship was limited to a maximum term of 6-months, a term-limit which was never transgressed.

The one important formal limitation – and here is the characteristic most clearly distinguishing this dictatorship from all others that have ever existed – was the six-month term of office for the dictator was chosen. This length of time is explained by the fact that the early Romans fought only in the summer. It was a restriction on the dictatorship that was never transgressed, by force or by law. Indeed, another convention of the Roman constitution bound the dictator to abdicate his office immediately his particular piece of business had been successfully terminated. Machiavelli wrote of the Romans he so greatly admired that 'if any of them arrived at the dictatorship, their greatest glory consisted in promptly laying this dignity down again.'[80]

Rossiter also discussed how gradual changes to constitutional government, including the normalization of unaccountable executive power, can ultimately become permanent features of politics in that society.

[I]nherent in the constitutional employment of dictatorial institutions is the simple fact that changes less than revolutionary, but nonetheless changes, will be worked in the permanent structure of government and society. No constitutional government ever passed through a period in which emergency powers were used without undergoing some degree of permanent alteration, always in the direction of an aggrandizement of the power of the state.[81]

America, from 1945 to the post-9/11 world is a case in point. Rossiter concludes by noting that wars, tyrannies, and political transformations of the 20th century reconfirm that,

the age-old phenomenon of constitutional dictatorship has reached the peak of its significance. Men are just as willing today as they were in ancient Rome to renounce their freedom for a little while in order to preserve it forever.[82]

The sociocultural phenomenon of Trump's electability seems to vindicate Rossiter's observation. A segment of the pro-Trump electorate appears to be reasonably open to renouncing some of our constitutional freedoms, although in light of the content of Trump's campaign pledges, it remains unclear how such sacrifices will translate to the preservation of order in our society.

Rossiter Redux after 9/11

Balkin and Levinson resurrected Rossiter's constitutional dictatorship thesis in their 2010 *Michigan Law Journal* article of the same title, and applied it to Bush administration policies after 9/11. Balkin and Levinson observe how symptoms of dictatorial rule can manifest democratic politics during times of emergency. Updating Rossiter's thesis, Balkin and Levinson define Constitutional Dictatorship as follows:

> a system (or subsystem) of constitutional government that bestows on certain individuals or institutions the right to make binding rules, directives, and decisions and apply them to concrete circumstances, unhindered by timely legal checks to their authority. When they act according to this right, they act clothed with all of the authority of the state. These persons or institutions, however, are subject to various procedural and substantive limitations that are set forth in advance. These may include the time and/or circumstances in which they may exercise authority, the subjects over which they may exercise their authority, and specific means for implementing their decisions.[83]

The constitutional law scholars suggest that a Constitutional Dictatorship is constitutional because government is still limited when its form of political organization waxes dictatorial. Once the democracy becomes a dictatorship, the dictatorial powers

> come with various limits prescribed by law and enforced by institutional structures. The dictator exercises power according to constitutional procedures that bring the dictatorship into being, end it, and structure its scope and reach.[84]

This assessment is theoretically plausible, but also Panglossian to a fault. Turning an intellectual blind eye to the historical fact of a century of American selective illiberalism is not a persuasive way for Balkin and Levinson to suggest that a theoretical possibility may present a workable paradigm of dictatorial rule in democratic government.

Historically, from Pinochet to Rajapakse, Pol Pot to Sani Abacha, the only rule that dictatorships have vigilantly followed is the rule of lawlessness. For instance, in America's War on Terror, the Bush administration did not and was not required to comply with *limits prescribed by* any *law* prior to perpetrating torture in counterterrorism investigations, such as waterboarding Khalid Sheikh Mohammed 183 in Guantanamo Bay detention facilities. The rule of constitutional law was given lip service, honored in the breach, and used by Washington to democratize illiberal policies. The American politics of global counterterrorism unfolded on the honor code through executive unilateralism, a code that Bush construed as discretionary. After 9/11, the Bush administration committed torture, ordered the Office of Legal Counsel to create a legal theory to constitutionalize it post hoc, and then bet that the policy would never be subjected to meaningful judicial review. In hindsight, the Bush administration got it right, more or less.

In this regard, Balkin and Levinson do warn us that normalizing governmental policy during times of emergency is a risky business:

> [I]f one is willing to break laws in urgent circumstances, this creates a precedent for breaking them again where

the urgency is more controversial (or nonexistent); moreover, it encourages political leaders to retain unconstitutional norms even after the emergency has passed. What starts as emergency measures may become normalized.[85]

This status quo is a slippery slope. The absence of meaningful checks and balances in a system of government invariably seduces governmental leadership to abuse power. Balkin and Levinson elaborate:

Although the rhetoric of emergency is the standard justification for dictatorship, dictatorial powers may not be connected to any real emergency. Moreover, even if dictatorship is initially justified by emergency, it may continue after the emergency is over. In this way, dictatorial powers may become normalized. Executive officials, noting the ability of emergency to focus the public's attention, and to route around the unusual impediments to reform, may find themselves in quest of ever- new emergencies to justify the continuation of their authority.[86]

On balance, Balkin and Levinson wholeheartedly endorse Rossiter's constitutional dictatorship thesis. They conclude that a Cincinnatus-style constitutional dictatorship within American constitutional democracy is what is best for America. In doing so, they probably did not anticipate the reasonable possibility of an unpredictable presidential candidate like Donald Trump contending competitively in presidential elections. Nevertheless, like Machiavelli,

Hamilton, and Lincoln, the constitutional law scholars explain to us in the 21st century that episodes of the American government's transition to constitutional dictatorship are advantageous to American power rather than debilitating. Such transitions can provide Washington the decisional autonomy, force, latitude, and efficiency required to extirpate threats to national security with decisive force on short notice when time is of the essence..

Balkin and Levinson conclude with presumably comforting words:

> Dictatorships can occur even in democracies, if the public gives officials unchecked powers ... It should be obvious from this definition that many elements of republican government could be seen as "dictatorial" to the extent that they endow government actors with essentially unreviewable discretion to set policy and execute it immediately with the force of law.[87]

The authors "firmly" support the positive role that constitutional dictatorship in American democracy.

> We place ourselves firmly on the side of Hamilton and the great Florentine statesman of the *Discourses*. We cannot leave the growth of republics to chance and circumstance; one must design systems for emergencies in advance to head off problems before they occur ... We forget the lessons of Machiavelli, revived in the past century ... The notion of "constitutional dictatorship" may seem at first a contradiction in terms, but it is a reality that every modern democracy (like every ancient one)

must eventually face. Whatever problems may attend the design of emergency powers in a constitutional democracy, it would be even worse to slide into patently unconstitutional dictatorships; the past century alone has witnessed far too many examples.[88]

Constitutional dictatorships may seem viable in theory. But the practice of politics – in particular American politics in national security and foreign affairs – often diverges from the prescriptions of theory. In this regard, Balkin and Levinson are right to warn us. The details of a constitutional democracy's *slide into the politics of a patently unconstitutional dictatorship are* where the devil sleeps. It is also in such details where a Trump presidency could discover the political space to remorselessly inflict unstoppable, unmitigated, irreparable, and unconstitutional harm and havoc to American citizens at home and the global citizenry abroad.

7

The Neoimperial Presidency

imperialism *im-pir-ē-ə-li-zəm*\
(n.) 1. a policy of extending a country's influence through diplomacy or military force; 2. rule by an emperor

---

With G.O.P nominee Donald Trump nipping at the gates of the Oval Office of the international community's most powerful democracy, Trumpophobia is no paranoid delusion. It is as real as our taxes or rush hour traffic, the secret drone strikes in Mali and Yemen or the covert CIA extraordinary renditions in Ethiopia and Somalia and black sites in Poland and Afghanistan. Trumpophobia is arguably the only sensible reaction to Trumpism in a rational political society that is faithful to liberal values and the rule of law, to its genesis as a Nation of immigrants and a color-blind constitutional order.

Trump wholeheartedly repudiates such commitments. If his campaign pledges in 2016 convert to policies in 2017, Trump seems to be maturing into a textbook anti-Cincinnatus. Like Caesar, Trump will likely prove to be an addict for abusing power rather than respecting it, usurping more of it in favor of relinquishing excesses. For a moment, consider that if a president Trump were to use the Trump Card, and sanction policies like banning Muslims or deporting 11 million illegal immigrants, these policies may prove impossible to slow down or stop through normative political processes. One such variable abetting this brand of presidential politics is the increasingly imperial character of the American presidency, a trend that has intensified since the end of World War II.

The Imperial Presidency of Yore

The term 'imperial presidency' was coined back in the 1970s in a book of the same title written by the American historian, Arthur Schlesinger. As timely now as then, the *Imperial Presidency* was published in the aftermath of a historically unprecedented chain of cataclysmic events including the Vietnam War, the Iran/Contra Affair, and the Watergate scandal, the aggregate weight of which wrought ruin on the Nixon administration and American society.

The embryo of the American imperial presidency was conceived much earlier than Nixon's presidential election in 1968, arguably starting with the Truman administration. The Cold War replaced the vacuum in international politics left by the end of World War II in 1945. As America metamorphosed from an ordinary democracy to a liberal superpower during this period, a bipolar competition with the Soviet Union on a global battlefield from Cuba to Angola intensified.

Our limited government grew. Executive power expanded. Executive policy globalized.

Additionally, the Truman administration also created the

CIA through the National Security Act of 1947, a legislative act that gave birth to the American national security establishment, an institution that has relentlessly expanded in size and power for over half-a-century now. As the national security establishment grew, power continued to concentrate in the executive branch while weakening the checks and balances within our system of constitutional government that were once capable of limiting the exercise of that power.

As a result, Washington – including the executive branch and the American presidency – grew strong. We, the people, and the democratic controls on Washington became weak. In a nutshell, this state of affairs created Schlesinger's imperial presidency. As Schlesinger explains, the imperial presidency is not really about classical imperialism like British colonial rule in India, Belgian rule in the Congo, or French Indochina. Schlesinger's concept of an imperial presidency is more about accountable representative politics in American constitutional democracy:

> I had written the *Imperial Presidency* in the latter days of Richard M. Nixon. The American Constitution, the book argues, envisages a strong presidency with an equally strong system of accountability. When the constitutional balance is upset in favor of presidential power and at the expense of presidential accountability, the presidency can be said to be imperial.[89]

As Schlesinger describes, national security has always been the pretext for executive unilateralism that exacerbates the politics of non-accountability, from the days of Nixon to the post-Obama years of American politics:

The all-purpose invocation of 'national security,' the
insistence on executive secrecy, the withholding of
information from Congress, the refusal to spend funds
appropriated by Congress, the attempted intimidation
of the press, the use of the White House itself as a base
for espionage and sabotage directed against the political opposition — all signified the extension of the
Imperial Presidency from foreign to domestic affairs.
Underneath such developments there could be dis-
cerned a revolutionary challenge to the separation of
powers itself.[90]

Schlesinger also ponders a cure for this plight that has
afflicted the American system of constitutional democracy
since the end of World War II.

The American democracy must discover a middle
ground between making the President a czar and making
him a puppet. The problem is to devise means of recon-
ciling a strong and purposeful Presidency with equally
strong and purposeful forms of democratic control. Or,
to put it succinctly, we need a strong Presidency — but a
strong presidency within the Constitution.[91]

The benighted pattern of imperial presidential politics in
American statecraft that Schlesinger described did not end
with Nixon. To the contrary, the pattern has exacerbated
and intensified since Nixon. Today, it breathes through the
constitutional anarchy of anti-supremacy politics and likely
will continue to do so under a Trump presidency. At its
core, the institution of the American presidency has

become powerful to the extent that its accountability to the people or the Constitution has become discretionary. Further, after Nixon's preemptive resignation in 1973 to avoid impeachment proceedings, the pattern of executive usurpation of power has expanded from the Ford administration through the Obama presidency, easily adapting the entrenched foreign policy reflexes of Cold War-era thinking to the post-9/11 world, interchanging America's ideologized fear of the red communist with the brown terrorist.

Indeed, from the heavens, if Alexander Hamilton has been looking down on us at least from Nixon to November 8th 2016 and beyond, he would be giving Schlesinger a high five, while telling us, "I told you so." In the *Federalist No. 8,* Hamilton warned ominously against the executive usurpation of power:

> It is the nature of war to increase the executive at the expense of the legislative authority.[92]

In the *Federalist No. 75*, Hamilton advocated against the concentration of executive power in a constitutional democracy:

> The history of human conduct does not warrant the exalted opinion of human virtue which would make it wise to commit interests of so delicate and momentous a kind as those which concern its intercourse with the rest of the world, to the sole disposal ... of a President of the United States.[93]

Each of the 18th century fears of Hamilton has become a 21st century *fait accompli*. In hindsight, Schlesinger was a Cassandra character. Our presidency was imperial during the Cold War and in many ways it still is during the War on Terror. Political scientist Andrew Rudalvige comments further in his book, *The New Imperial Presidency: Renewing Presidential Power After Watergate*, publishing after 9/11 in 2006:

> [P]residents have regained freedom of unilateral action in a variety of areas, from executive privilege to war powers to cover operations to campaign spending. There are meaningful parallels between the justificatory language of the Nixon administration and that of our most recent presidents: each stressed the notion of 'inherent' presidential power, the broad sweep of constitutional 'rights' of the office. This development would have endured even had President Bush failed of reelection in 2004. The default position between presidents and Congress has moved toward the presidential end of the interbranch spectrum – and irreversibly so.[94]

The imperial presidency that has ossified into a veritably permanent component of the American social contract from Nixon to Bush II, has been extended by the Obama administration, and will be at the disposal of this presidential election's winner. However, more disconcerting is a scenario where we have an imperial presidency *and* an imperial president who holds the Trump Card, unencumbered by normative sources of self-restraint like law or morality, consent or the threat of accountability for unconstitutional or unconscionable projections of power.

Our living constitutional order has adapted to sustain rather contain this treacherous path of structural political transformation in the form and function of our government. If we are able to see the form and function of our government through the fog of political and legal orthodoxy, in the post-9/11 world, what seems increasingly evidence is that the American presidency is no longer imperial.

The modern American presidency is neoimperial.

The Neoimperial Presidency

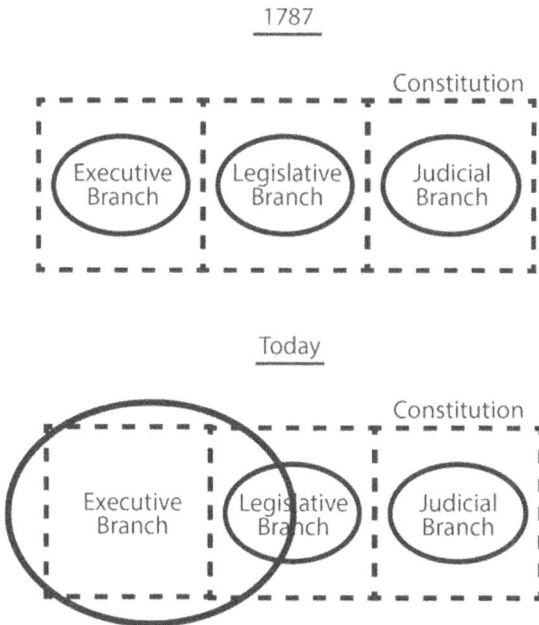

Fig. 12: The American Neoimperial Presidency: 1787 and Today

A surreptitious form of state-building, the polymorphous ripple effects of the New Deal catalyzed a chain of policy decisions after the Great Depression that gained momentum in the 1930s and 40s and ultimately transformed the basic form and function of American government. The New Deal-era political climate, one that continues today in certain respects, gradually built up the American administrative state, brick by brick, agency by agency. In particular, this process enlarged the size and power of the executive branch, as conceptually shown in Figure 12.

It all started around the New Deal era under the Roosevelt administration when Congress began delegating its powers -- essentially outsourcing its duties – to entities outside of the legislative branch, enlarging the size and function of the federal government. Slowly, our constitutional blueprint began to buckle and mutate. Our limited government got bigger. Aspects of the government's legislative and policy-making authority gradually changed hands from Congress to newly minted and expanding administrative agencies, like the Food and Drug Administration (FDA), Environmental Protection Agency (EPA) and the Internal Revenue Service (IRS). More recent examples of Washington building out the administrative state include the flurry of new agencies created in response to the 2008 Financial Crisis or the still expanding, quasi-Leviathan black box ecosystem of the national security establishment.

A fruit of informal constitutional change, this redistribution of power within our system of government from a three-branch political design to one with an administrative state too is zero-sum. As the administrative state grows, the political branches of government weaken. In this sense,

Congress deliberately chose to become weaker by passing
the buck on policy decisions to various executive administrative agencies. Accordingly, the executive branch –
including the presidency – became stronger and started
legislating in areas Congress typically would.

As a result, our contemporary branches of government
– the executive, the legislative branch, and the judiciary are
still co-ordinate within our constitutional order. However,
from the perspective of workable government, they have
inarguably become separate *and* unequal branches. In light
of congressional delegation, judicial restraint, and the rise
of the post-New Deal administrative state, the executive
branch of modern America – the one that a president
Trump would inherit upon electoral victory – has become a
branch that considerably overpowers the others two
branches in the contemporary age of American politics.

In this way, *through* the rise of the administrative state,
the American imperial presidency, once singularly anchored in the executive branch, evolved into the American
neoimperial presidency, with institutional roots in all three
branches of American government.

While Schlesinger's concern after Nixon was the presidency's imperial powers, today, the American neoimperial
presidency's global and often secret projection of unilateral
power flows through a variety of channels, including the
presidency, the executive branch-centric national security
establishment, and a small world network of administrative
agencies to which Congress has delegated the power to
make law and policy.

To this extent, America's neoimperial presidential politics are harder to check and balance since they are carried

out not by one imperial branch within the constitutional order but rather by an incestuous ecosystem of intertwined institutions: the presidency, the executive branch, and the administrative state.

The conundrum that we, the people, face now is not that our presidency can act imperially within our constitutional order. The American presidency can act neoimperially within the constitutional order, both on its own *and* by proxy through administrative agencies in ways that are not checked or balanced by an acquiescent legislature or deferential judiciary. The backbone of these changes to our governmental structure is a product of informal constitutional change and was born of the New Deal constitutional struggle between the Supreme Court in one corner of the ring and Roosevelt administration and Congress in the other. They tussled over the issue of whether it was proper and constitutional for Congress to delegate its powers to non-legislative entities, like the presidency.

In hindsight, Congress won that argument by fiat. To be sure, the prohibition of congressional delegation – called the doctrine of nondelegation – is vital to our Constitution's separation-of-powers scheme. For instance, way back in 1690, John Locke wrote in his seminal work, *A Second Treatise on Government,*

> [t]he Legislative cannot transfer the Power of Making Laws to any other hands. For it being a delegated Power from the People, they, who have it, cannot pass it over to others.[95]

The Supreme Court upheld the Locke's view almost two centuries later in *Field v. Clark* (1892):

> That Congress cannot delegate legislative power to the President is a principle uniformly recognized as vital to the integrity and maintenance of the system of government ordained by the Constitution.[96]

In fact, the doctrine of nondelegation *is* the separation boundary that separates our three branches of government in our Constitution's tripartite structural scheme, recently expounded upon by Justice Thomas in his concurring opinion in *Department of Transportation v. Association of American Railroads* (2015):

> The Constitution does not vest the Federal Government with an undifferentiated 'governmental power.' Instead, the Constitution identifies 'three types of governmental power and, in the Vesting Clauses, commits them to three branches of Government. Those Clauses provide that '[a]ll legislative Powers herein granted shall be vested in a Congress of the United States,' Art. I s. 1, '[t]he executive Power shall be vested in a President of the United States, Art. II s. 1 cl. 1, and '[t]he judicial Power shall be vested in one supreme Court, and in such inferior Courts as the Congress may from time to time ordain and establish,' Art. III s.1. These grants are exclusive.[97]

In hindsight, the jurisprudential tide of nondelegation in the American constitutional order turned during the Great

Depression. Congressional delegation became constitutionally permissible. When it did, from Roosevelt to Obama, we began to gradually see the selective break down of our constitutional separation-of-powers scheme that otherwise divides our one government into three branches. The onset of this process is generally traceable to the Supreme Court's 1928 landmark ruling, *J. W. Hampton, Jr. & Co. v United States,*[98] which held that despite textual provisions in the Constitution, Congress did have an *implied power* to delegate its duties to the executive branch so long as it provided an 'intelligible principle' to aid the executive branch in carrying out said congressional duties. The Supreme Court holding in *J. W. Hampton* effectively created a legislative-executive branch merger in particular policy domains.

Since then, our administrative state has run off the rails.

Building on top of the *J. W. Hampton* precedent, another landmark Supreme Court case, *Chevron U.S.A. v. Natural Resources Defense Counsel, Inc.*[99] (1984) delivered another deathblow to the Constitution's separation of powers scheme by creating the *Chevron* deference doctrine that instructs court's to defer to administrative interpretations of law. In other words, if an executive administrative agency believes a policy to be lawful, the court should defer. *Chevron* deference effectively created a judicial-executive branch merger in particular policy domains.

To recap, our system of constitutional government has three branches: the executive, legislative, and judiciary. *J. W. Hampton* created legislative-executive merger in 1928. *Chevron* deference created judicial-executive merger in 1984. If you do the constitutional math, in 2016, we now have a single institutional entity in our government – the executive administrative state – that is performing all three functions of our tripartite system of constitutional government. It legislates for itself. It determines the legality of its own conduct for itself. It then executes policies based on its own legislation and legality determinations.

Recall that even if limited to specific policy domains like foreign affairs or national security, this sort of governmental model is the exact form of political organization that Madison repudiated in *Federalist No. 47:*

> The accumulation of all powers, legislative, executive, and judiciary, in the same hands, whether of one, a few or many, and whether hereditary, self-appointed, or elective, may justly be pronounced the very definition of tyranny.[100]

Although we still call it democracy, Madison would have called it tyranny. While Congress has remained docile and acquiescent of this culture of constitutional politics that continues to delegate congressional duties to the executive branch, Supreme Court Justices have objected over the years. Justice Scalia dissenting in *Mistretta v. United States*[101] (1989) lamented:

> It is difficult to imagine a principle more essential to democratic government than that upon which the doctrine of unconstitutional delegation is founded: except in a few areas constitutionally committed to the Executive Branch, the basic policy decisions governing society are to be made by the Legislature. Our Members of

Congress could not, even if they wished, vote all power to the President and adjourn *sine die.*[102]

More recently, Chief Justice Roberts dissenting in *City of Arlington, Texas v. Federal Communications Commission* (2013) warned that

> [a]lthough modern administrative agencies fit most comfortably within the Executive Branch," they combine legislative, executive, and judicial power. 'The accumulation of these powers in the same hands is not an occasional or isolated exception to the Constitutional plan; it is a central feature of modern American government.'[103]

What does this all mean now and after November 8th?

The powers that be in Washington have become more powerful and institutionally entrenched than we may have thought. The executive administrative states lives on. It is nurtured by a normalized congressional culture of delegation that without conscience subverts the Constitution's separation of powers scheme while eroding the doctrine of nondelegation into dead letter law. All branches of government are co-conspirators in this outcome, one way or another.

Resting on the jurisprudential edifice of the 1928 *J.W Hampton* precedent and post-1984 *Chevron* deference doctrine, Congress keeps outsourcing its duties to executive administrative agencies. The judiciary infrequently adjudicates in such areas and when it does, can't form a majority to stop it. The executive branch, salivating for

more power, offers no objection to its own aggrandizement, and accordingly has swelled in size, autonomy, and
power since the Great Depression, and through World
War II, the Cold War, and War on Terror. This has created
a complex balkanized administrative apparatus in which a
legislative-executive-judiciary merger of power in our
government has already occurred and is consolidated. This
administrative apparatus has been at the informal disposal
of the American presidency. It is also an essential part of
the nation-state's institutional machinery and national
security establishment but not clearly accountable to any of
the branches of government or the people.

In parallel to its Art. II Commander-in-Chief powers,
the American neoimperial presidency acts through this
standalone entity of the administrative state. The administrative state functions like a loyal, obsequious sidekick that
breathes under the neoimperial presidency's wing, like
what Robin is to Batman, what Biden was to Obama, and
what Mike Pence may be to a president Donald Trump.

Imagine. All of this power and autonomy may soon rest
with Donald Trump. That is frightening.

One of the reasons the constitutional concerns raised by
the national security administrative state remains unana-
lyzed in the American public square is because
administrative law is dry, dense, and complicated. Roman
jurist Tacitus remarked once, *the more corrupt the republic, the
more numerous the laws*. Whether or not we consider Washington as corrupt, we *do* have a *lot* of laws, especially
administrative ones. No single citizen, lawyer, judge, politician or even president-elect for that matter can reasonably
comprehend them all. As big government replaced limited

government, and positive law replaced natural law, our rule of law has become a labyrinth. This labyrinth also includes an ecosystem of political and constitutional norms that persist due to the government's systematic non-enforcement of particular existing laws or non-legislation of new rules to regulate particular types of conduct.

The labyrinth also includes our national security administrative state. Robert Knowles provides a succinct overview:

> A massive amount of government activity takes place entirely in secret ... The United States has a bifurcated administrative state. There is an ordinary administrative state, in which agencies must solicit and consider public comments before issuing rules with the force of law. And there is a national security administrative state, in which agencies may choose to issue the same sort of rules without first publishing them and without soliciting or receiving public comments, while some rules may be kept entirely secret.[104]

The Administrative Procedures Act (APA) is the primary statute governing laws for agency conduct. A national security exception to the APA and Executive Order 12,866 together enable agencies active in the policy domains of foreign affairs and national security to write secret laws shielded from public scrutiny or congressional oversight. Knowles elaborates:

> [T]he national security exception ... is alive and well. It is an expression of, if not the foundation of, the national

security administrative state ... [I]n our administrative law's web of national security exceptionalism, the APA's notice-and-comment rulemaking exception stands out because it applies to every agency, in times of war and peace. And it does most work to strip national security rulemaking of the key features that are believed to ensure democratic accountability, transparency, and legitimacy.[105]

Although musing of political life in ancient Rome, Tacitus was right about a political society having *too* many laws. Here, we have an administrative state mired in administrative laws and authorized to write secret laws itself. What would or could a Trump presidency do with such an administrative apparatus? Troubled, Journalist Fred Hiatt sums up the harrowing concerns raised by the confluence of the American neoimperial presidency, the election of Trump as president, and our growing administrative state in his *Washington Post* article entitled, *Why Justice Ginsberg's Trump Derangement Syndrome is a bad sign*, published on July 15, 2016:

[W]hen judges declared that Obama had gone too far with his attempt to legalize millions of illegal immigrants, he stood down. He was bitterly disappointed, no doubt, but acceded to the judicial decision. What if a president decided to ignore such a decision? What if he had appointed an attorney general, a budget director, a border chief or other bureaucrats eager to abet such defiance? Imagine, for example, that judges told a President Trump that he could not turn the Southwest border region into 'a police state,' which the executive

director of the American Civil Liberties Union forecast ...
would be the result of Trump's plan to deport 11 million
undocumented immigrants. Imagine that Trump and
his administration continued building camps anyway.
Given the contempt that Trump has expressed for the
judiciary, and the ignorance he has displayed of the
Constitution, that scenario is not so far-fetched.[106]

If Donald Trump is elected as President come January 20th
2017, we can reasonably forecast a constitutional crisis by
Christmas of 2017 if he makes good on at least one of his
campaign promises.

While comforting in theory, the doctrine of
nondelegation doctrine has become a feeble prophylactic
in practice against the executive usurpation of power. It no
longer polices the separation-of-powers boundaries in our
system of constitutional government. While plausibly giving
pause to a Cincinnatus-like president-elect, nondelegation
will have a negligible impact on a Trump administration.
Such developments in our constitutional order amplify the
clear and present danger of Trumpism.

Historical perspective provides clarity. Our system of
constitutional government has changed significantly
between 1776 and the post-9/11 world. Congressional
delegation would likely have been viewed as a threat to the
Constitution's separation of powers scheme during the
Founding-era, spurned as manufacturing a conflict of interest
in our government structure in which ambition is intended to
counteract ambition, as Madison put it. What was once
viewed as a conflict of interest in the constitutional order is
now viewed as a synergy for executive governance.

Since the Founding-era, the *tao* of modern American governance supposes that the judiciary checks executive branch policies through the threat of review, actual review, or invalidation, and by doing so, constitutionalizes such policies. When the Nation is not submerged in crisis, the judiciary often does. But within a crisis, when government policy is often secret and extraterritorial, the judicial check is chronically illusory in practice, and all bark and no bite, as it were. In the practice of American politics, other than a familiar script of hypothesis and counter-hypothesis in public debate, constitutionality determinations of American policy during a crisis and in the domains of national security and foreign affairs are rarely decided in a court of law. Instead, the executive branch decides them for itself in the court of public opinion and by fiat through executive action. Now, rather than the judiciary, it is a Constitution that the neoimperial presidency and national security establishment are expounding, having legitimized an array of illiberal policies from Truman to Obama, including torture and extraordinary rendition, drone warfare and force-feeding hunger strikers.

This slow metamorphosis has vitiated the principled grip of checks and balances on government policy, ineluctably weakening we, the people, while vitalizing the *powers that be* in Washington.

In the vacuum left by the degeneration of checks and balances in our system of government, political cultures of implied trust and implied self-restraint have emerged to maintain the constitutional equilibrium in politics we are accustomed to. This new political culture places executive policy on the honor code.. This arrangement tends to work so long as we elect a Cincinnatus-like president, who will vigilantly respect the rules of implied trust and self-restraint that attach to contemporary norms of presidential politics. The arrangement will break down and foment constitutional crisis when we elect an Caesar-like president who will do as dictators do when granted access to unlimited, unaccountable power.

Abuse it.

8

(Let's) Make America Great Again

purgatory *pər-gə-tȯr-ē*\
(n.) a place or state of suffering inhabited by the souls of sinners who are expiating their sins before going to heaven.

Friends, Americans, countrymen, lend me your ears and your conscience, your common sense and the better angels of your nature.

November 8th nears. As the clock ticks down to presidential election day, it seems appropriate to adapt a well-known soothsayer's premonition from the days of Caesar: *Beware the ides of November.*

Incessant news reportage of this presidential election has swallowed the American public square whole. The sheer ubiquity of the Trump brand has made *not* thinking about Donald Trump a Sisyphean task. And yet, if we can see through the fog of Trumpism to the other side of the election, we might notice that decisive, paramount pre-election issues have been left unreported or neglected at the margins of debate.

Perilous conditions in American politics set the stage for the ides of November: a neoimperial presidency, an elastic post-9/11 constitutional order with no meaningful checks and balances to tame it, and Donald Trump – a black swan candidate who may fill the Oval Office vacancy in the White House come January 20th 2017.

Ultimately, we must decide on a forward course for our Nation. Day by day, America's electoral fork in the presidential road crystallizes more and more, increasingly molded by a morass of either-or choices: Clinton or Trump, female or male, the promise land or purgatory, the stay-the-course candidate or a multibillionaire with a cause, presidential politics as usual or the imminent risk of a crippling constitutional crisis in the reasonably foreseeable future. If elected, Trump could turn our Constitution, a charter of liberties, into the doormat of an elected dictator who twists democratic politics into elective despotism. From Pol Pot to Al-Assad, Pinochet to Rajapakse, and Sani Abacha to Saddam Hussein, the life of republics has drilled home one lesson over and over: in any organized society, it only takes one strong man to turn democracy into dictatorship, a Camelot into Sodom and Gomorrah. In America's Camelot, such a strong man could be Donald Trump.

Love or loathe Donald Trump, the fact that Trumpism has found an organic electoral base in American society reveals that there is a lot more at stake in this election than which nominee wins. The electoral outcome will resolve whether Trump or Clinton change their domicile to the White House. The electoral outcome will not solve bigger structural and constitutional problems in our democratic political process unearthed by this election season. The biggest structural and constitutional problem exposed thus far is the absence of an effective GOP gatekeeping function to prevent the nomination of an unpredictable candidate for an office that wields illimitable, unaccountable power. Moreover, the electoral outcome will not cure the propensity of public debate in American society to permit the important national issues that surface during a campaign to fade from the ephemeral fore of national concern to its blurry fringes where political moments in popular memory routinely vanish into the archives of historical amnesia.

Such is the state of our Union.

So, take another breath. Take it *all* in, again, knowing what we do now our Constitution and GOP presidential nominee Donald Trump.

At this late stage in the election season, it is probably advisable to avert our solitary focus on Trump's psychological (un) fitness to be our 45th American president. Voters on both sides of the divisive issue have formed their beliefs already, ones which are likely impervious to change from *more* information and analysis about Trump's mental stability. To be sure, even if Trump were to be clinically diagnosed with a psychosis like Neurotic Personality Disorder, unlike in American criminal law, Not Electable by Reason of Insanity (NERI) is not a viable plea or remedy available to disqualify him from contending for the American presidency. Even if it were, it's just too late. The punditry's laser-focused fixation on Trump's mental instability has enriched pre-election public conversations but is also a form of denial from the traumatic shock experienced on July 19th when Trump secured the official GOP nomination.

Painful as it may be, it is better to accept the electoral facts before us. Trump is in the presidential race. Trump is the alternative to Clinton. And come January 20th 2017, all of us may be addressing Donald Trump as President Trump. And yet, still, an unnerving question mark persists beneath the electoral political momentum pulling us to November 8th, one that strikes a simpler non-psychological chord.

How did Trump even get in the race? Is this the party of Lincoln? Really?

Antwerp Diamond Heist

Trump slithered into the race in part because he tapped into a reservoir of latent xenophobia and generalized rage that percolates beneath the cosmopolitan veil of the American multicultural melting pot. Trump was also able to enter the race in substantial part due to the GOP's failure to groom and then nominate an adequate pool of vetted, electable presidential candidates, a necessary precondition for our bipartisan system of competitive electoral politics to work. In each presidential election, *both* parties need to *authentically* back candidates they support so that voters actually have a choice.

As we have discovered together as a Nation, the GOP ran out of presidential petrol sometime in 2016. We, the people, ended up with Donald Trump as the official GOP nominee on July 19th. At its root, this nomination reflected a grave failure in the GOP's gatekeeping function. The role of nominee gatekeeping is sacrosanct to the integrity of presidential elections in our two-party democracy. To this extent, the magnitude of the GOP's failure in nominating Trump has no precedent in its 163-year life of the GOP, founded by anti-slavery Whigs in March 1854. The scope of the GOP failure is best conveyed by analogy: the Antwerp diamond heist a.k.a. the heist of the century.

The Antwerp Diamond Center is located in Belgium's gem district. It is the three-block epicenter of the global diamond trade where multimillions of dollars in shiny stones exchange hands daily. The Antwerp Diamond Center has an underground, vault that is protected by multiple levels of security, including: a three-ton one-foot thick steel door, infrared heat detectors, a seismic sensor, Doppler radar, a magnetic field, a private security force, and a lock with 100 million combinations.[107] The vault was considered impenetrable up until Valentine's Day in 2003.

On the weekend of February 15-16th 2003, Leonardo Notarbartolo and five members of the Italian crime ring *La Scuola di Torini*, broke in to the vault and stole $100 million dollars in loose diamonds, gold, jewelry, and other spoils. When Belgian police arrived on the scene, the thick steel door was ajar, and the vault was empty.[108] Belgian police still struggle to definitively explain how Notarbartolo broke in. Although Notarbartolo was able to break in, at least the valuables held in the Antwerp Diamond Center were protected by a vault with multiple layers of security to keep jewelry thieves out.

The American presidency is the gem of the American constitutional order. Where were the GOP's security measures on its official nomination of a presidential candidate? The GOP's vault was unprotected. Donald Trump essentially walked straight through the ajar gate as an inexperienced outsider, a differentiating attribute he has now woven into his campaign sloganeering. Indeed, Charles Krauthammer observed of Trump's ascent:

> A candidacy that started out as a joke, as a self-aggrandizing exercise in xenophobia, struck a chord in a certain constituency and took off. The joke was on those who believed that he was not a serious man and therefore would not be taken seriously. They — myself emphatically included — were wrong.[109]

One might even say that Notarbartolo's heist was as improbable as Trump's GOP nomination. While different in nature, parallels exist between the two. Any criminal or underdog is an accidental disciple of guerilla warfare. As either, the odds are against you, be it stealing diamonds or running for president as an untested outsider. To overcome power asymmetries *and* win, you *must* strike the system where it is weak *and* unregulated.

Al Qaeda did this on 9/11. Lehman Brothers, Morgan Stanley, and Goldman Sachs did this with subprime mortgages in the 2008 global financial crisis. Notarbartolo and the Italian crime ring *La Scuola di Torini* did this back in the 2003 Antwerp Diamond heist.

Trump is doing it now. Let's not forget, by proxy, Sara Palin -- yes, the incoherent, charismatic, and self-proclaimed hockey mom-cum-pit bull with lipstick – did it in 2008 when she almost became the Vice President of the United States of America. This is worth repeating. *Sara Palin almost* became the Vice President of the United States of America.

America is still a superpower in many ways, and yet we continue to witness this peculiar, dysfunctional pattern in presidential election politics. It makes our presidential election more dangerous than elections in other democracies like Botswana and Brazil, Iceland and India, Hong Kong and Honduras. Why? In our globalized world, the America's sphere of national interest is global – there is no inch of Earth it does not touch. American policy in national security and foreign affairs is also projected globally, and affects everyone, everywhere. In this respect, the presidential election of Donald Trump would not only affect California and New York, but also Copenhagen and Nairobi, Caracas and New Delhi. America's de facto superpower status scales Trumpophobia, which would be a localized electoral virus in any other nation-state, into an issue of potentially global relevance.

Surprisingly, to date, only one aspect of the compound fear of Trumpophobia has received meticulous analysis in the mainstream media: the fear of Trump as an individual, namely his unsavory repertoire of neurotic quirks, from racial prejudice to the reflex to hurl vitriolic ad hominem attacks at any source of critique of his candidacy. The other aspect of that compound fear – the focus of this book – is just as important. It is the public fear of Trump as a president-elect who, branding the Trump Card, would occupy the helm of the American neoimperial presidency, an executive institution of our constitutional government that has insidiously become endowed with unlimited, unaccountable, unilateral power.

The post-1945 arc of informal constitutional change is the proximate cause of this structural transformation in our political society. Even under the presidential leadership of relatively more tame and civilized individuals like a

Bush or Obama, the American presidency has proven capable of sanctioning a sordid spectrum of policies. They include: assassination by drone strikes in Yemen, torture in Cuba, wars of choice in Iraq, abductions in Somalia, military intervention in Libya, surrogate warfare in Syria, and a planetary net of dragnet surveillance that covers the laptops and smartphones of the Tamil auto-rickshaw driver in Jaffna as much as the twenty-something start-up multi-millionaire in Silicon Valley.

Donald Trump may wield all of this power soon.

Today, Trump's thumbs counterattack critiques with unscripted tempests of vociferous tweetstorms, tempered recently by the straitjacket of Teleprompters and election campaign management. It begs the question, what will Trump do when he has the military arsenal of the post-9/11 national security establishment at his fingertips? One of our society's great democratic virtues is that that *any* natural-born citizen can become president. In the flip side of that coin lurks a once dormant vulnerability: *any* natural-born citizen can become president, including a multibillionaire real estate mogul with a sixth grade vocabulary.

Pinpointing Trump's *actual* endgame courts an elusive quest that may ultimately prove unanswerable prior to November 8th. Consider for instance, that Trump registered a federal trademark for "MAKE AMERICA GREAT AGAIN" (Reg. No. 5020556), filing his application a month after announcing his presidential candidacy. This type of intellectual property strategy is a sound advice to protect and monetize a brand. But, it makes you further question Trump's fundamentals.

We return to the question -- *how did Trump even get in the race?* Is Trump running for president or commercializing a product? The answer may very well be both. Of course, Trump lifted the campaign slogan from Ronald Reagan's 1980 Presidential campaign slogan, "Let's Make America Great Again."

*Fig. 13: A Button from Ronald Reagan's 1980
Presidential Campaign*

Paraphrasing 19th century French philosopher Joseph Maistre, every Nation gets the government it deserves. By extension, every democracy deserves the presidency it elects. But, is it fair to apply this maxim to us now, when one party in our two-party system – the GOP – has failed to put forward a sane, vetted, electable presidential candidate.

When the psychological driver of voting decisions is controlled more by whom one is voting *against* rather than *for,* the proper line of inquiry is not do we deserve a particular elected administration. It is more basic. Why do we deserve this electoral system? In elections, a choice of one is no choice at all. The GOP's official nomination of Trump highlights an unstated assumption of American presidential politics. In a two-party political system, each party must vigilantly perform its own gatekeeping function to vet and nominate its *best* candidate, rather than *any* candidate. When one party fails to do so, electoral politics in that two-party system collapses.

Mirror, Mirror, on the Wall

In American presidential elections, the winners celebrate. The losers commiserate, plunging into a four-year purgatory in which they make vows to return with a new politics, revised slogans, and replenished campaign donors in the next presidential election cycle. However, in *this* election, the electoral outcome should only be one part of the story.

Trumpism is another part of that story, one that tells us more about ourselves than either presidential candidate. Down the road in 2017, we can reasonably anticipate three possible electoral outcome scenarios if we continue to look in this political mirror. Each outcome raises national issues that we, the people, may need to grapple with post-election, irrespective of which presidential candidate wins.

In Scenario One, Trump wins by any margin, a couple ballots or a landslide. Here, our Nation must confront some hard political truths. Primarily, we would need to accept that our multicultural melting pot is not colorblind or post-racial. Rather, it incubates popular grievances rooted in racist, xenophobic public sentiment that simmer beneath a cosmopolitan veil of pluralism. Said otherwise, we, the people, are *not* a Nation of immigrants; we still see ourselves as a *white*

Nation *with* immigrants, naturalized or not, illegal or not, even if we elected a black president in 2008. Further, since no substantive checks and balances reliably regulate the immense power wielded by the modern American neoimperial presidency, the election of Trump as president would have immediate foreign policy implications of global scope starting in Q1 of 2017, stretching from Somalia to Cuba, Israel to Pakistan, Russia to China to Brazil.

In Scenario Two, Trump loses a competitive election to Clinton by a slim margin.

This is the quintessential close call. With Trump losing, a Clinton presidency presents fewer risks to the state of the post-election Union. However, such a close race reveals the work remaining in extirpating the corrosive role of invidious racism and Anglo-Saxon nativism from American politics. Trump's ability to galvanize an electoral base through race-fueled demagogy rebuts the premise that American society desegregated into a colorblind utopia. It clearly has not if Trump can surge to the official GOP nomination on a policy platform that promises to ban Muslims and deport Mexicans.

In Scenario Three, Trump loses by a landslide to Clinton. Although risky like Russian roulette is, this electoral outcome would vindicate the American democratic process and the role of public debate in adequately fleshing out presidential candidates when the nominating parties don't. Here, in America, any natural-born citizen can run for president, even a multibillionaire real estate mogul with a sixth grade vocabulary, the media will vet such a candidate during the campaign season, and the voters will choose wisely on election day.

In Scenario One, Scenario Two, or Scenario Three, the question to ask is not *can* we elect Donald Trump as president. We can. America is a democracy. The question to ask is can the Constitution constrain Donald Trump once he assumes office? If past is prologue in American constitutional politics, the uncomfortable truth is probably not.

We, the People

While the media focal point of elections habitually fetishizes the presidential candidates, it is easy to forget that democracy is about the people more so than the candidates. After all, the vector of public opinion is the oxygen of democratic power. A presidential candidate's electability simply reflects our common aspirations.

To this extent, the focal point in this election is really *on us*. The term "we" in "we, the people" refers to *all* of us. We are *one* Nation *united* under *one* government under *one* rule of constitutional law. Quite familiar with the incurable scars a divided society can inflict on the human soul, Martin Luther King articulated the sacrosanctity of a united people poignantly in his landmark missive, *Letter from Birmingham Jail*:

> I am cognizant of the interrelatedness of all communities and states ... We are caught in an inescapable network of mutuality, tied in a single garment of destiny. Whatever affects one directly affects all indirectly.[110]

King's words are salient to remember given the divisive, xenophobic nature of and rage-fueled demagogy woven in to Trump's electoral campaign platform.

Our indivisibility as a people is the womb of our invincibility as a Nation. It always has been.

To this extent, the fibers of our social fabric are resilient but not indestructible, reifying the dream of colorblind unity while acknowledging the realities of racial division. Our social fabric remains united even during presidential election seasons which routinely tribalize America's multicultural melting pot into segregated vats of voters defined by socioeconomic determinants such as race, religion, and tax bracket, all visualized in interactive touch-screen maps on CNN and Al Jazeera.

At the same time, as we also rediscover every four years, such divisions are also what make us a beautifully diverse mosaic of neighbors and strangers, soldiers and civilians, tied in a single garment of destiny. Today, "we, the people" is a phrase that is culturally tethered to American soil while also transnationally transcending territorial boundaries. Enclaves of diasporic communities pepper our national fabric from Chinatown in New York to the Somali enclaves in Minnesota, the Spanish-speaking suburbs of Texas to Indian communities in New Jersey. All are equally American, whether Democrat or Republican, of the right or left, rich or poor, white collar or blue, white or non-white, man or woman, young or old, gay or straight, Judeo-Christian or Muslim, from our upwardly mobile gated communities to our gang-laced ghettoes, from sea to shining sea, from July 4, 1776 to January 20, 2017 and beyond.

Whatever our skin color or religious conviction, we are *all* American. We *all* must choose a candidate on election day. Once we vote, Washington's policies are carried out in our name, the good and the bad. Our ballots democratize these policies and our tax dollars bankroll them. If we vote Trump in to the Oval Office, we will also be responsible for a Trump administration's policies. If we vote Clinton in to the Oval Office, we will also be responsible for a Clinton administration's policies.

Trump or Clinton, the formulation and sustainability of these policies, some more non-representative than others, generally will flow from concentrations of executive power that have pooled in Washington in the neoimperial presidency, buttressed by the political cultures of judicial deference and congressional abdication that have collapsed our Constitution's separation of powers scheme. Anti-supremacy politics has filled the vacuum left by a debilitated system of checks and balances in our constitutional order that has witnessed Washington grow powerful and we, the people, become weak through the Cold War and War on Terror.

As this pattern of American statecraft has unfolded surreptitiously since Truman and to the detriment of our republic, order has slouched into anarchy, constitutional democracy into ad hoc constitutional dictatorship, a system of laws into a system of men. The continued force of *Curtiss-Wright* only adds fuel to the fire. During times of emergency, American presidents from Truman to Obama have generally done what they wanted, when they wanted, using whatever means they wanted, all without the need for prior congressional authorization or the fear of post hoc judicial review or accountability. Within such circumscribed zones of government policy, the American president unabashedly walks, talks, feels, and functions like a benevolent dictator.

Indeed, the Supreme Court recognized this deleterious trend early on. Justice Jackson, in the famous Steel Seizure case, *Youngstown Sheet & Tube Co v. Sawyer[111] (1952)*, decided under the Truman administration during the Korean War, commented on structural transformations to the American Presidency in his concurring opinion:

> [I]t is relevant to note the gap exists between the President's paper powers and his real powers. The Constitution does not disclose the measure of the actual controls wielded by the modern presidential office. That instrument must be understood as an Eighteenth-century sketch of a government hoped for, not as a blueprint of the Government that is. Vast accretions of federal power, eroded from that reserved by the States, have magnified the scope of presidential activity. Subtle shifts take place in the centers of real power that do not show on the face of the Constitution.[112]

On January 20, 2017, all of this unchecked concentration of executive power might rest in the unwise hands of Donald Trump.

The Lives of Others

Greek statesmen Pericles once observed,

> What you leave behind is not what is engraved in stone monuments, but what is woven into the lives of others.

If we overlook Trump's many business achievements that

have engraved their distinctive mark on American popular culture, from Trump Towers to the reality-television show *The Apprentice*, what the GOP presidential nominee has woven into the lives of others in this election campaign has *not* been customer satisfaction. It has been fear and xenophobia, nativist division and incivility, alpha-male narcissism and rage-fueled demagogy.

Nevertheless, Trump, the Colossus, tromps onward, as the ides of November approach.

In the lives of voters, choices must be made, often based on imperfect information. So, let's start with what we do know. The Trump Card, a cast iron sword of Damocles hanging over the fate of our Constitution, *is real.* The yin and yang of Trumpism and Trumpophobia *is real.* The slow metamorphosis of the American constitutional order through informal constitutional change into a form of government that accommodates paroxysms of constitutional dictatorship under the aegis of an energetic executive branch *is real.* The American presidential need for a Cincinnatus and not a Caesar in the Oval Office *is real.* The American neoimperial presidency – along with its unchecked, unbalanced powers and administrative apparatus - *is real.* And the compound fear of a Trump administration – the fear of Trump as an individual entangled with the fear Trump as a president – *is real too.*

What is happening in America?

What has happened to America already?

Market forces invariably make the agile pendulum of mainstream media coverage fickle, its analytical spotlight swinging between fresh revelations of new facts about Trump and chronic retreats into a narcissism of small differences that make us, the consumers of news content, repeatedly lose perspective of the bigger picture. If we, the people, can manage to mentally pierce the partisan smog of electoral data and spin, we might be able to make out the silhouette of a multibillionaire real estate mogul with a sixth grade vocabulary who has insinuated himself into America's presidential election.

Will 2016 be remembered as the year that Trump *ran* for president or *became* one?

The choice between Trump and Clinton is still ours to make. Based on the political conditions we know of and the imperfect information we do have, we might conclude that in this presidential election, *we* – meaning all of us -- *need* a Cincinnatus-like president to occupy the Oval Office between 2016 and 2020. America is a democracy. We *can* elect a Caesar if we so choose to but should be aware of the grave, avoidable risks implicated by that choice. A Caesar-like president can easily abuse power and morph into a Trojan horse that foments constitutional crisis, like Nixon did in Southeast Asia, like Bush did after 9/11, or how Obama surreptitiously did through his use of executive orders in domestic policy and surrogate warfare abroad in places like Yemen and Syria.

During the Cold War and War on Terror, bombs and bullets from policies in our foreign affairs and national security are administered by an American presidency that remains de facto ballot-proof in the inter-election period. A Trump presidency would be too, until 2020.

However, all is not lost. The alarm bells of Trumpophobia have begun to sound, even at this late hour. Quietly and resolutely, voices of dissent and reason water an anti-

Trump revolution in bloom on both sides of the aisle as November 8th nears.

Can Clinton capitalize? Or will her campaign improprieties, like a handful of lies about private e-mail servers and her dissemination of Benghazi-related classified information as Secretary of State, metastasize into a cancerous Achilles' heel that causes her to lose the race? If she can't capitalize, the American voter is in a bind.

Consider the alternative. Is Donald Trump reasonably capable of sound presidential decision-making during times of normalcy, let alone emergency? It is unclear. What Donald Trump knows how to do without question is successfully manage corporations and generate wealth. But, politics and business are not the same. A democratic nation-state is not run like a big corporation. Diplomacy is more than return-on-investment deal-making, even in a capitalistic democratic society such as ours.

Such is the tortured state of our electoral choices. Looking forward, the Trump-Clinton debates may fall well short of the Pacificus-Helvidius debates between Hamilton and Madison. We should expect more vituperative mudslinging than political prophecy, to say the least. Be that as it may, the choice facing voters between Trump and Clinton is unenviable, resonating as quick and simple for some and excruciatingly self-flagellating for others. In all cases, the issues implicated by this voter decision transcend the mundane histrionics of everyday electoral politics. The issues, from voting in a female president to banning Muslims from American soil, cut to the core of American self-identity and test the raw substance of our moral fiber, our intangible sense of what sort of social contract we seek for our ourselves and what sort of society we gift to our grandchildren's grandchildren.

The unique electoral moment we inhabit is tormenting, but electric with democratic life. Its asphyxiating omni-presence is sure to fade fast into oblivion by the ides of November when the 45th president of the United States of America has already been chosen. Like a cold machete, the electoral moment also pierces to the pulsating soul of modern America in the breast of every citizen who will cast a ballot from Brooklyn to Honolulu, Houston to Bethesda. The moment reminds us of the closing stanza from English poet William Ernest Henley's *Invictus:*

> It matters not how strait the gate,
> How charged with punishments the scroll,
> I am the master of my fate,
> I am the captain of my soul.[113]

Although Henley wrote *Invictus* whilst battling tuberculo-sis, the inner-strength he craved from his hospital bed echoes a century later in different circumstances: Trumpophobia in the 58th quadrennial American presi-dential election. Trumpophobia has gripped and polarized the Nation as November 8th nears, pitting white against non-white, citizen against immigrant, Republican against Republican. *Invictus'* spirit of self-reliance is quintessential-ly American, reverberating through the tides of history, from the armed skirmishes at Lexington and Concord into the post-9/11 world. This spirit *is* the lifeblood that still vitalizes our arteries of democratic self-government.

From Brooklyn to Honolulu and Houston to Bethesda,

in American democracy, we are still the masters of our shared fate. We, the people, are still the captains of our collective soul.

You and I, even as citizens may be strangers, even if we live on the same block or in the same apartment building, work for the same company or served in the same infantry unit. Yet, our individual fates are bound on November 8th when we vote. We are on that day, as Martin Luther King once said, intimately part of an *inescapable network of mutuality, tied in a single garment of destiny.*

However, our patriotic sense of propinquity for our Founding-era is no alibi for our selective ignorance of the neoimperial impulses of our presidency today, or how Washington has worked in practice since the Cold War. This holds true whether or not Donald Trump is on the GOP ticket now or is referred to as President Trump come January 20th 2017.

Self-rule implies self-accountability. Making America great again occludes a politics of force and fear, the touchstone of Trump's election platform. Making America great again starts with the reflective choices that we, the people make about the sort of society and culture of constitutional self-government we strive to nourish, here at home, here and now.

The luxury of indifference is no longer one our Nation can afford. Election day is November 8th.

Who are you voting for?

Notes

Chapter 1

[1] See www.macmillandictionary.com/us/buzzword/entries/black-swan.html (Date Accessed: 31 Aug. 2016). See also generally: Taleb, Nassim Nicholas, *The Black Swan: The Impact of the Highly Improbable,* Random House Trade Paperbacks, 11 May 2010.

[2] See http://shakespeare.mit.edu/julius_caesar/julius_caesar.1.2.html (Date Accessed: 08/31/2016). The quote referenced is from Act 1, Scene 2 of William Shakespeare's *The Life and Death of Julius Caesar* .

[3] See http://www.gallup.com/opinion/polling-matters/187652/one-four-americans-dislike-presidential-candidates.aspx. (Date Accessed: 09/04/2016)

[4] See http://www.rollingstone.com/politics/news/how-america-made-donald-trump-unstoppable-20160224. Taibi, Matt. "How America Made Donald Trump Unstoppable." *Rolling Stone* . 14 Feb. 2016. (Date Accessed: 31 Aug. 2016)

Chapter 2

[5] 347 U.S. 483 (1954)

[6] See https://www.washingtonpost.com/news/the-fix/wp/2016/08/02/president-obama-just-went-off-on-donald-trump/. Cillizza, Chris. "President Obama just turned his criticism of Donald Trump up to 11." *Washington Post* . 2 Aug. 2016. (Date Accessed: 31 Aug. 2016)

[7]www.salon.com/2016/03/28/fox_news_charles_krauthammer_unloads _on_donald_trump_hes_obviously_a_good_candidate_but_hes_going_to _be_terrible_for_the_country/. Kaufmann, Scott E. "Krauthammer unloads on Donald Trump." *Salon* . 28 Mar. 2016. (Date Accessed: 15 Aug. 2016)

[8] http://www.nytimes.com/2016/08/05/opinion/campaign-stops/i-ran-the-cia-now-im-endorsing-hillary-clinton.html?_r=0. Morell, Michael J. New York Times. 5 Aug. 2016 (Date Accessed: 15 Aug. 2016)

[9] See http://www.politifact.com/wisconsin/article/2016/jul/13/what-ruth-bader-ginsburg-said-about-donald-trump/. Kertscher, Tom. "What Ruth Bader Ginsberg said about Donald Trump." *Politifact*. 13 Jul. 2016. (Date Accessed: 15 Aug. 2016)

[10] See http://www.cnn.com/2015/12/23/politics/young-jeezy-don-lemon-interview/. Zaru, Deena. "New Jeezy video 'Sweet Life' spotlights criminal justice reform." CNN. 18 Jan. 2016. (Date Accessed: 15 Aug. 2016)

[11] See https://www.washingtonpost.com/opinions/gop-senator-why-i-cannot-support-trump/2016/08/08/821095be-5d7e-11e6-9d2f-b1a3564181a1_story.html?utm_term=.0b90bff71777. Collins, Susan. "GOP Senator Susan Collins: Why I cannot support Trump." *Washington Post* . 8 Aug. 2016. (Date Accessed: 15 Aug. 2016)

[12] 299 U.S. 304 (1936)

[13] Ibid. at 320, 321.

[14] See http://www.economist.com/news/leaders/21573106-appeal-populist-autocracy-has-been-weakened-not-extinguished-hugo-ch%C3%A1vezs-rotten. (Date Accessed: 09/03/2016)

[15] See https://en.wikipedia.org/wiki/Vladimir_Lenin. (Date Accessed: 09/03/2016)

[16] See http://www.theatlantic.com/magazine/archive/1954/10/when-lenin-returned/303867/. Crankshaw, Edward. "When Lenin Returned." *The Atlantic* . October 1954 Issue. (Date Accessed: 09/02/2016)

[17] See http://www.nytimes.com/2016/07/19/opinion/trump-is-getting-even-trumpier.html?_r=0. Brooks, David. "Trump is Getting Even Trumpier!" *New York Times* . 19 Jul. 2016. (Date Accessed: 09/01/2016)

[18] See https://www.washingtonpost.com/opinions/global-opinions/trumps-shallowness-runs-deep/2016/08/03/f7311b20-58d3-11e6-831d-0324760ca856_story.html?utm_term=.73a7ecd7d9bf. Will, George F. "Trump's shallowness runs deep." *Washington Post* . 03 Aug. 2016. (Date Accessed: 09/01/2016)

[19] See https://www.washingtonpost.com/opinions/donald-trump-and-the-fitness-threshold/2016/08/04/b06bae34-5a69-11e6-831d-0324760ca856_story.html?utm_term=.1fb32f3f0924. Krauthammer, Charles. "Donald Trump and the Fitness Threshold." *Washington Post* . 04 Aug. 2016. (Date Accessed: 09/01/2016)

[20] Ibid.

[21] See http://www.nytimes.com/2016/08/05/opinion/campaign-stops/i-ran-the-cia-now-im-endorsing-hillary-clinton.html. Morell, Michael J. "I Ran the C.I.A. Now I'm Endorsing Hillary Clinton." *New York Times* . 05 Aug. 2016. (Date Accessed: 09/01/2016)

[22] See http://www.constitution.org/fed/federa51.htm. Madison, James. "The Structure of Government Must Furnish the Proper Checks and Balances Between the Different Departments." Independent Journal. 6 Feb. 1788. (Date Accessed: 15 Aug. 2016)

Chapter 3

[23] See http://www.merriam-webster.com/dictionary/dictator. (Date Accessed: 31 Aug. 2016)

[24] Walker, Leslie J. *The Discourses of Niccolo Machiavelli* . Rutledge, 2006, pp. 289-290.

[25] Ibid.

[26] Machiavelli, Niccolo. *Discourses on Livy* (Julia Conway Bondanella & Peter Bondanella trans., Oxford Univ. Press 1997) (1531), pp. 95.

[27] Ibid.

[28] See http://www.constitution.org/fed/federa70.htm. Hamilton, Alexander. "The Executive Department Further Considered." *Independent Journal* . 15 Mar. 1788. (Date Accessed: 31 Aug. 2016)

[29] Ibid.

[30] Jaffa, Harry V. A New Birth of Freedom: Abraham Lincoln and the Coming of the Civil War . Rowman & Little Field Publishers, 2004. P. 361.

[31] Rossiter, Clinton L. Constitutional Dictatorship: Crisis Government in the Modern Democracies . Princeton Univ. Press: 1948

[32] Ibid.

[33] Department of Justice Brief, *John Doe I, et al., v. George W. Bush, et al.* , U.S. Court of Appeals, 1st Circuit No. 03-1266(2003).

[34] Declassified CIA Document referred to as the 'Doolittle Report". Doolittle, James H. *Report on the Covert Activities of the CENTRAL INTELLIGENCE AGENCY* , 1954.

[35] 376 U.S. 254 (1964).

[36] Kommers, Donald P. American Constitutional Law: Essays, Cases, and Comparative Notes, Volume 1. Rowman & Littlefield Publishers, 2009. p. 781.

[37] See
https://www.theguardian.com/theguardian/2007/sep/07/greatinterviews
1 (Date Accessed: 09/02/2016)

[38] See https://www.washingtonpost.com/news/the-
fix/wp/2016/03/03/the-fox-news-gop-debate-transcript-annotated/. (Date
Accessed: 08/31/2016).

Chapter 4

[39] See http://www.constitution.org/fed/federa51.htm. Madison, James.
"The Structure of the Government Must Furnish the Proper Checks and
Balances Between the Different Departments." *Independent Journal* . 6
Feb. 1788.

[40] 5 U.S. 137 (1803)

[41] Ibid.

[42] 258 U.S. 433 (1922).

[43] Bickel, Alexander J. *The Supreme Court and the Idea of Progress* . Yale
Univ. Press, 1978. pp. 20-21.

[44] Bolingbroke, Henry. *Bolingbroke: Political Writings* . Cambridge Univ.
Press (1997). pp. 88-89.

[45] 60 US 393 (1857).

[46] 410 U.S. 113 (1973)

[47] 548 U.S. 557 (2006)

[48] 558 U.S. 310 (2010)

[49] 133 S. Ct. 2675.

[50] 135 S. Ct. 2584.

[51] Strauss, David A. *The Living Constitution* . Oxford Univ. Press, 2010.
pp. 2-3

[52] Ibid., at 139.

[53] Balkin, Jack M. *Living Originalism* . Belknap Press, 2011. pp. 24-29.

[54] Ibid.

[55] Ibid.

[56] Jack M. Balkin, *The Roots of the Living Constitution* , Boston Law
Review, Vol. 92, 2012. pp. 1135-1137

[57] Amar, Akhil R. America's Unwritten Constitution: The Precedents

and Principles We Live Bay . Basic Books, 2012. pp 33-37.

[58] See http://www.cnn.com/2016/01/14/politics/larry-tribe-donald-trump-ted-cruz-gop-debate/. Krieg, David. "Who is Larry Tribe and why are Trump and Cruz talking about him?" *CNN* . 15 Jan 2016. (Date Accessed: 31 Aug. 2016)

[59] Tribe, Lawrence H. *The Invisible Constitution* . Oxford Univ. Press, 2008. pp. 21-22

[60] Eskridge, William N., Ferejohn, John. *A Republic of Statutes: The New American Constitution* . Yale Univ. Press, 2010. pp 1-3.

[61] Ibid., at 2.

[62] Ibid., at 6.

[63] Koh, Harold. The National Security Constitution: Sharing Power after the Iran-Contra Affair . Yale Uni. Press, 1990, pp.68-69.

[64] Ibid.

[65] Ibid., 117-119

[66] Griffin, Stephen M. *American Constitutionalism: From Theory to Practice* . Princeton Univ. Press, 1996. Pp. 6-11

[67] Ibid.

[68] Ibid. at 13-16.

[69] Ibid. at 57.

Chapter 5

[70] See http://www.constitution.org/fed/federa15.htm. Hamilton, Alexander. "Insufficiency of the Present Confederation to Preserve the Union." *Independent Journal* . 1 Dec. 1787. (Date Accessed: 31 Aug. 2016)

[71] See http://www.providenceforum.org/spiritoflibertyspeech. (Date Accessed: 31 Aug. 2016)

Chapter 6

[72] Ibid. at 2.

[73] Ibid. at 4-5.

[74] Ibid. at 7.

[75] Ibid. at 16.

[76] Ibid.

[77] Ibid. at 25.

[78] Ibid. at 19-23

[79] Ibid. at 21.

[80] Ibid. at 23.

[81] Ibid. at 294-299

[82] Ibid. at 13.

[83] Sanford Levinson, Jack M. Balkin. *Constitutional Dictatorship: Its Dangers and its Design* , Minnesota Law Review, Vol. 94 2010, p. 1805.

[84] Ibid. at 1807

[85] Ibid. at 1800

[86] Ibid. at 1809.

[87] Ibid. at 1806.

[88] Ibid. at 1866.

Chapter 7

[89] Schlesinger, Arthur J. *The Imperial Presidency* . Mariner Books, 2004. pp. ix-xi

[90] Ibid. at xxvii

[91] Ibid. at xxviii

[92] See http://www.constitution.org/fed/federa08.htm. Hamilton, Alexander. "The Consequences of Hostilities Between the States." *New York Packet* . 20 Nov. 1787. (Date Accessed: 31 Aug. 2016)

[93] See http://www.constitution.org/fed/federa75.htm. Hamilton, Alexander. "The Treaty-Making Power of the Executive." *Independent Journal* . 26 Mar. 1788.

[94] Rudalvige, Andrew. The New Imperial Presidency: Renewing Presidential Power after Watergate . Univ. of Michigan Press, 2005. p. 261.

[95] See http://www.constitution.org/jl/2ndtr11.htm. (Date Accessed: 02 Sept. 2016)

[96] 143 U.S. 692 (1892)

[97] 575 U.S. ___ (2015), Docket No. 13-1080.

[98] 276 U.S. 394 (1928)

[99] 467 U.S. 837 (1984)

[100] See http://avalon.law.yale.edu/18th_century/fed47.asp. Madison, James. "The Particular Structure of the New Government and the Distribution of Power Among its Different Parts." *New York Packet* . 1 Feb. 1788.

[101] 488 U.S. 416

[102] Ibid.

[103] 569 U.S. ___ (2013), Docket No. 11-1545

[104] Robert Knowles, *National Security Rulemaking* , Florida State University Law Review, Vol. 41, 2014. pp 884-889

[105] Ibid. at 904

[106] See https://www.washingtonpost.com/opinions/why-justice-ginsburgs-trump-derangement-syndrome-is-a-bad-sign/2016/07/14/e5392352-493a-11e6-acbc-4d4870a079da_story.html?utm_term=.492daffc94ec. Hiatt, Fred. "Why Justice Ginsberg's Trump Derangement Syndrome is a bad sign." *Washington Post* . 14 Jul. 2016 (Date Accessed: 09/02/2016).

Chapter 8

[107] See http://www.wired.com/2009/03/ff-diamonds-2/. Davis, Joshua. "The Untold Story of the World's Biggest Diamond Heist." *Wired.* 12 Mar. 2009 (Date Accessed: 09/02/2016)

[108] Ibid.

[109] See https://www.washingtonpost.com/opinions/donald-trump-and-the-fitness-threshold/2016/08/04/b06bae34-5a69-11e6-831d-0324760ca856_story.html?utm_term=.3ee393f1e5aa. Krauthammer, Charles. "Donald Trump and the Fitness Threshold." *Washington Post* . 04 Aug. 2016. (Date Accessed: 09/02/2016)

[110] See http://www.theatlantic.com/politics/archive/2013/04/martin-luther-kings-letter-from-birmingham-jail/274668/. (Date Accessed: 09/02/2016)

[111] 343 U.S. 579 (1952)

[112] Ibid.

[113] See https://www.poets.org/poetsorg/poem/invictus. (Date Accessed: 09/02/2016)